2021 B. Jacob
Copyright 202

Cover Design
Grant Mallory
Son-In-Law to Brian Jacob

Published by
Passages & Prose, LLC.

ISBN: 9798513517429

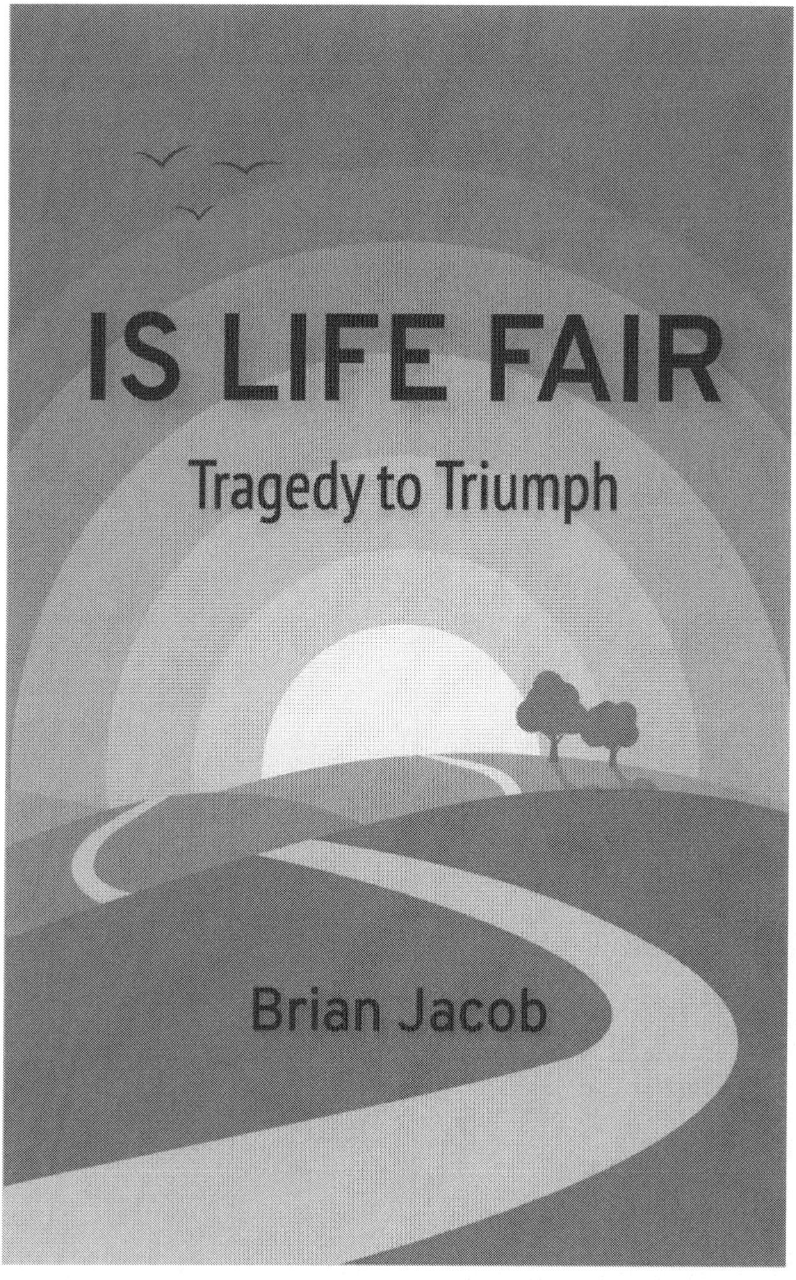
IS LIFE FAIR
Tragedy to Triumph
Brian Jacob

Table of Contents

Acknowledgment

I would like to express my sincere appreciation to all the people in my life that have helped me in dealing with an extremely limiting physical disability. The courteous strangers who open doors when I approach, the gracious coworkers who have always accepted me and recognized my physical but not mental limitations, the friends who knew and remembered me when I was young and healthy, and the friends who were not afraid to get to know me later despite my disability. To Lillie Leonardi for supporting me in the publishing of this book. My family, especially my mother and father, who always loved and supported me throughout their lives and sacrificed much to make sure I was cared for. Last but not least, my three favorite gifts from God: my son Brady, my daughter Maria, and my loving wife, Jamie, for her pledge to stand by me through good and bad while always motivating me to continue living life to the best of my ability.

Introduction

Often after tragedy, people contemplate, *How could this happen?* and *Why me?* During my times of confusion and searching for an answer I often felt that life was not fair. Is life fair? I guess this is the underlying question to be answered by the reader after reading my personal life story and coming to grips with their own situation. No one ever guaranteed me that life was fair, but it is an assumption that you make when you are young and the world ahead seems promising and bright. I was blessed to have been born to loving parents in a middle-class home with several brothers and sisters. Like most people that I knew, I grew up with much ambition to better myself and find a loving spouse who could share all of my dreams. My future looked promising as I entered college and imagined having a professional career and family of my own someday. A tragic accident occurred in my life resulting in quadriplegia and ultimately a completely different outlook for my future. Would my future be fair if I were confined by a wheelchair and all the limitations of a spinal cord injury? This book tells the story of my fears, cheers, setbacks and accomplishments. Is life fair? Hopefully this question will be answered and the reader will be inspired by my outlook on life after dealing with these trials and tribulations.

A Life Changing Moment

I remember the evening well. November 15, 1978 was just like any other fall day in Southwestern Pennsylvania; the weather was chilly and wet. I contemplated what jacket to wear before I left my house for wrestling practice. I volunteered as a coach for the junior program at the local YMCA where I had wrestled as a youngster. I enjoyed wrestling and working with young kids, teaching them the sport. I decided to wear my ski jacket. I liked it and being that the weather was getting cooler, it was appropriate for the night. It might seem strange that I had given so much thought to this selection, but my recollection of this emphasizes the amount of detail that I recall regarding that time and evening.

I was 19 years old and was planning to pursue a career as a chiropractor. This profession seemed to suit me well because I was athletic and very interested in human anatomy. I felt that this would be a career that I could truly enjoy while helping others. I had always liked participating in and watching sports, including Little League baseball, youth swimming and diving, football, track, boxing and wrestling. (As my sister would often remind me, I was a jock.) Of these, I enjoyed wrestling the most because it was a sport that someone like myself who was not really tall enough for basketball or large enough for football could excel in based upon being matched evenly within a weight class. As a young boy I was often overlooked in team sports because of my size, so wrestling was ideal for me.

With wrestling practice starting soon, I grabbed my car keys and headed out the door for the New Kensington YMCA. On the brief 10-minute drive, I kept thinking about the final that I had taken that morning. It was for the last college course that I needed to be admitted to a chiropractic college. I also remember worrying about my younger brother who was starting to drift into trouble. I felt obligated to watch over him as an older brother should. I had passed up a date that night with a girl who was very interested in me; I was more interested in wrestling. She had contacted me earlier and wanted me to meet her. In hindsight, I should have accepted. I'm sure it would have resulted in a less dramatic evening.

When I arrived at the YMCA, I ran up the steps to the second floor gymnasium where the wrestling mats were kept. I rushed into the facility, hanging my jacket and keys on a volleyball post, never thinking that I would never put on that jacket or drive my car again.

Practice was scheduled to start soon and we needed to roll out the wrestling mats and tape them. Preparing the mats for wrestling practice was a ritual that required the assistance of several guys. I had been rolling out wrestling mats since I had started the sport as a ten-year-old here at the YMCA.

Moe Guin was the activities director and also coach of the team that I had wrestled on when I first got interested in the sport. He was a muscular, middle-aged black man who had always shaved his head before it was considered chic to do so. We all loved Moe because he had a special way with kids. We feared his physique but respected him because we knew that he cared very much about all of us. We knew that he loved wrestling, and it was typical for him to spend time wrestling on the mats with us even after practice was finished. He was much stronger than any of the youth wrestlers and we openly admired his strength and greatly appreciated his caring personality and devoted coaching.

Moe had developed quite a following with his youth program and it was helpful to have more than one coach there for these sessions. It was my responsibility to make sure that the kids were learning the right techniques and staying focused on practice. It was a busy evening in the gym with kids on the mat and several mothers sitting along the wall watching. Our practice lasted over an hour, then everyone cleared off of the wrestling mats so that we could begin to roll them up.

A couple of guys that were friends of mine from high

school, Pat and Gino, had shown up to play basketball after the mats had been cleared and practice was over. I remember hearing the basketballs dribbling around the small gymnasium as Pat began to shoot hoops even though the mats had not been cleared yet. He had played basketball for our high school team but never wrestled. He was about 6' 3" and weighed over 200 pounds, lanky but surprisingly strong for his body frame. He often tried to show off whenever he had an audience and horseplay was an activity he was experienced in. Unfortunately for me, tonight there was an audience, a handful of people sitting off to the side of the gymnasium watching as the gym started to clear from wrestling and fill in for the upcoming basketball activities.

I had known Gino since junior high school and had always liked him. He had a contagious laugh and simple disposition. We had played youth football together and had many classes together throughout school. He had not left the area after high school or gone to college but instead worked as a carpenter. Unbeknownst to me, he'd decided that he wanted to wrestle with me even though he had limited wrestling experience and knew that my background and reputation as a college-level wrestler made it improbable that he would fare well. I recall that as I began to walk off the mat he grabbed me from behind and pulled me down to my knees. It was instinctive for me, as someone who had wrestled for many years, to try to escape when being held down on a wrestling mat. I could feel the weight of his body on my back and his strong arms around my waist and my arm. I knew that a Granby roll would easily free me from his confines. This was a move that I had first learned many years ago while attending a summer wrestling camp in Granby, Virginia. To complete this move I needed to tuck my head into my chest and roll over my shoulders while throwing my feet over and across my body. For only a split second are you in a vulnerable position but typically this move happens so fast that it is completed with no harm. In the split second that I began to roll across my shoulders with Gino behind me gripping tightly around my waist, I could hear the sound of Pat grunting loudly as he jumped on top of us. I tried to push back from the sudden weight of his hurling body and Gino's on top of me. It felt like a large gong had just been struck inside of me, its vibration permeating my body. I tried to scream at the moment of impact but was never able to get out any words. It was too late. I suddenly felt an extreme pain in my neck and nothing else.

As I laid motionless on my back, I realized that I was unable to move. I called out for Moe because I was scared and did not know what to do. Moe's face appeared above me as I stared up at the gymnasium ceiling, and I heard him asking me to squeeze his hand. I was unable to move my head because of the extreme pain in my neck but looked to my right to see his large black hand holding another hand. I quickly realized that the hand that he was holding was mine. I panicked at that point because I was completely paralyzed and had no feeling throughout my body. When you lose sensation in your body, you also lose your sense of where your body is positioned. You can only tell that you are lying down because you see the ceiling above you. I had gotten myself up off of the mat probably a million times throughout my many years of wrestling, but today I was not going to get up.

It seemed like a very long wait for an ambulance to arrive. There was a hush over the usually loud and energetic gymnasium. Moe and several others hovered around me while I lied there. He kept reassuring me that I would be fine but, despite his attempts of comfort, I really didn't believe him. I kept thinking about a friend of mine, Scott Doutt, who had sustained a spinal cord injury playing high school football just a couple years previously and had become confined to an electric wheelchair. I kept thinking to myself that I didn't want to end up like Scott. He and I had played youth football together and he was a talented athlete. I played quarterback and he was my best receiver. It was strangely coincidental that Moe had been our head football coach that year, and now here I was thinking about Scott with Moe at my side. When the paramedics arrived, they placed a hard collar around my neck which I could only move with extreme pain. They carefully rolled me onto a stretcher to take me out of the building. As they carried me down the steps, I remember being concerned about leaving behind my ski jacket with my car keys in the pocket.

My 1975 sky-blue Pontiac Firebird was parked across the street in an adjacent parking lot. This car was my pet and I loved driving it! I had always wanted a sports car and my father had bought it for me, slightly used, after we had an altercation. It was his way of trying to make amends with me for a bad situation. As a teenage boy, driving my car made me feel happy and gave me the sense of confidence that only a sports car can provide to a 19-year-old. I really enjoyed getting in it on a summer day, rolling down the windows, playing my favorite music and driving with no real destination in mind. Driving gives you a sense of independence and mobility that is not truly appreciated until you lose it. I often wish that I could still drive my Firebird and reconnect with that beautiful feeling of freedom.

The hospital was a short drive from the YMCA, so we arrived quickly. I had always had a small fear of hospitals and being rushed in on a gurney made me wish that there was still a chance of doing something differently so that I wouldn't end up in the emergency room, kind of like that feeling you get when you make a wrong turn while driving but quickly realize that it's too late to turn back. The doctor ordered x-rays of my neck and began to ask me how the incident occurred. I explained to him how my head was tucked into my chest and the force came down on me from behind. I recall him telling me that this was the most common position when someone gets a broken neck.

Wow, this was the first time that I had heard someone verbalize the situation that I had suspected but didn't want to hear. A broken neck was something that happened to other people but couldn't possibly ever happen to me. Maybe he was wrong. Maybe it was much simpler than that and could be fixed after a few days in the hospital. Maybe he was right and my situation was more traumatic than I'd hoped.

The hospital attempted to contact my parents who were recently divorced and living apart. My mother and my younger brother Tony were first to arrive and I remember being concerned for her because she was a recovering alcoholic and had just passed her first year of sobriety. I was worried that any type of extreme stress caused by this accident might result in her returning to her drinking and the many problems that affected our family as a result of it. She was always very affectionate to me and my siblings and was never shy about displaying her love for us or hiding her feelings. I could see the fear on her face when she looked down at me, and I was remorseful that she had to see me in this condition.

The doctor explained to us that they would need to place me in cervical traction in order to keep the bones in my neck from pressing together. I didn't understand his explanation but I was happy that they were going to start doing something to get me out of this hospital and back home as quickly as possible. They wanted to shave my head so that they could have a clear spot to drill two holes into the top of my skull. This was necessary so they could install hooks that would attach to the traction machine and gently pull the top of my head and help release pressure on my neck. I was horrified to think of my head being shaved. I had thick, wavy, dark hair that was fashionably long for a teenager in the mid-1970s. The thought of being seen with a shaved head was more concerning to me at that moment than the pain in my now-broken neck. In the 1970s it was uncommon to see anyone with a shaved head unless they were in the military, recently convicted or on the side of a Mr. Clean bottle. Strange that I was more concerned about my appearance than I was about this life-altering accident. After wasteful consideration, I decided that I would let them shave the top of my head where the screws would be inserted but requested they leave the remaining hair alone. At the time it seemed like a sensible decision, but later I wished that I had let them shave it all off because of the difficulty of cleaning my head and hair as a result of the blood that would drip from the drilled holes.

The initial plan was to drill two holes into the top of my head, but on the first try the spots were off-center and they needed to drill again next to the original holes. Although they used Novocaine to numb the area, I could feel the drilling into my skull, similar to what it feels like to have a tooth drilled, except that it vibrated my whole head. I ended up with four holes in the top of my head that are still sensitive and can be easily felt. I remember thinking then that I had more holes in my head than a bowling ball.

The physicians recognized that I needed to undergo surgery immediately. My mother consented for it to be performed at this local community hospital that was not experienced in performing this type of neurosurgery. I had grown up in this community and she felt that it was desirable for me to be at a hospital closer to my friends and family because I might be there for awhile. Her logic was based upon compassion, but realistically it was not the best decision for me. I might have had a more experienced neurosurgeon performing this delicate surgery and the follow-up care could have been more knowledgeable at a tertiary care center located in Pittsburgh. I don't fault my mother for making her decision because she did what she felt was best for me at that time. I am sure that she was very shaken being faced with the news that her teenage son had broken his neck and was currently completely paralyzed.

I had lost track of what time it was but realized that it must be getting late. I was scared because I had never had any type of broken bone or injury in my life up to this point. I was confused because I did not truly understand the medical logic or explanation of a spinal cord injury and why I was unable to move. I was anxious for the surgeon to do something because I couldn't imagine being in this condition for much longer and wanted to get it over with as soon as possible. As I continued to lie on the hospital cart looking up at the ceiling, I remember my mother and my little brother watching me with intense fear on their faces as the medical team rolled me out of the emergency room towards the operating room. I hated my little brother Tony seeing me like this. He had always looked up to me and I knew that I had become a surrogate father to him throughout my parents' divorce. He saw me as a strong big brother but now I lie there helpless and unable to move.

My Family

I was raised in New Kensington, Pennsylvania by my mother Jacqueline and my father Abraham, along with my four siblings Jeffrey, Jill, Amy and Tony. All five of us were born within a seven-year time span. Obviously, my father was very fertile and my mother was very energetic. Jeff was the oldest, born in 1957. I was second, born on December 23, 1958. Jill was third, born on the same day as me only one year later. Amy was fourth, born in June 1960. Tony, the last and affectionately referred to by my mother as the family baby, was born in 1963. Mom loved being a mother and had silly pet names for all of us. Jeff was Pooh-pooh (referring to Winnie the Pooh), I was Ninny, Jill was Dolly, Amy was Lizzie and Tony was Lambie Pie. All of these pet names were silly but they were a sign of my mother's affection.

Each of us are completely different and you would swear that we were all born from different parents. Although we have similarities in the way we look, we have very few similarities in the way we act. My older brother Jeff is the most outgoing and seemed to always have many friends around him. We spent lots of time together because we were fourteen months apart but were mostly schooled in the same grade. He had been held back in first grade by my parents.

Just prior to my accident, I had gone out and purchased a new snow ski outfit that I hadn't had a chance to wear yet. It was a beautiful black ski jacket with multiple colors striped around the shoulders along with a matching set of ski pants. I was eager for the ski season to start so that I could wear my new outfit on the slopes of the local Allegheny Mountains. While I was lying in the ICU, Jeff decided that he would borrow my new outfit because, as he later told me, "I figured you wouldn't be needing it". We both wore the same size clothing and he assumed that I wouldn't mind him taking my ski outfit for his needs. I was very angry with him because I had not accepted that my paralysis would be permanent and that instead I would be going skiing as planned in the near future. He didn't take my outfit to be mean, but it was a typical Jeff move that he made because he was the firstborn and always prioritized his own needs. I think that my accident affected him more than he displayed. I always knew that he loved and cared about me but his self-centeredness limited his emotional availability.

My sister Jill was very tiny in stature and I attribute this to why she was so combative in life. Even though we share the same birthday, we are completely different in personality and have never really gotten along well. She has many issues that I have never really understood but deep down I think that she is a very caring person and does care about me. At the time of my accident, she was a pregnant teenager. After the birth of her daughter, she asked me to be the godfather. I was honored to do this but very hurt months later when she gave the baby up for adoption. At the time Jill was very young and immature. As a single mother, she decided to let her daughter be adopted by our aunt and uncle living in Massachusetts.

My next youngest sister, Amy, was always a very kindhearted, free-spirited individual. Many of my friends referred to her as a hippie child. I got along with her, but we were also very different and didn't share many common interests. She made herself available to assist me often after my accident and I always felt that I could count on her if needed. She eventually moved away to California but I know that she loves me dearly and my accident was traumatic for her to accept. Amy was a pretty young girl and had many pretty young girlfriends. I always enjoyed when she invited her friends over to our house as this gave me an opportunity to meet them.

The youngest of these siblings was my favorite, Tony. He is about four-and a-half years younger than I am. We were roommates for many years because my parents separated Jeff and I due to our squabbling over bedroom cleanliness. I was always very particular about my clothes, my personal hygiene and my personal space. Tony and I shared a room together that I was able to keep clean and organized with him mostly because he was much smaller than me and I could force my hand when needed. I always loved Tony very much. He looked up to me and I enjoyed having a little brother. It is unfortunate that like most big brothers, Jeff and I teased him constantly. We should have been more sensitive. However, we always felt that we wanted him to grow up tough and not afraid of anyone. I guess it was our form of tough love. I think that my accident affected him the most because he was younger and always looked up to me. At that time our parents were recently divorced and he did not have much parental supervision. I had taken over as a quasi-father figure to him and my sudden absence was difficult for him to deal with.

We had a traditional family lifestyle for the times. My father was the breadwinner and worked three different jobs to make sure that we were financially comfortable. My mother was the homemaker, responsible for raising us five children and ensuring that we received much love and attention.

Mother was a very caring person who loved having children surrounding her. We were blessed to have been born to a woman who cared deeply about us. It was unfortunate that she began to have problems with alcohol when I was in my early teens. She used alcohol to escape from her problems and eventually ended up in an alcoholic rehabilitation center. She would spend nights drinking in her bedroom until she fell asleep on the bed oblivious to what was going on around her. She was a kind alcoholic who was easily taken advantage of when under the influence. This obviously led to us growing up in a household that lacked routine supervision. Five kids with lack of supervision is a recipe for trouble.

She tried hard to be a good mother. When I was a youngster, around the age of eight years old, she sewed Halloween costumes for all three of us boys. Jeff had an envious Batman costume that had a complete fitted hood, dark blue cape and bat emblem sewn on the chest. I was his sidekick Robin with a yellow cape, green mask and the capital letter "R" boldly displayed on the front of the red costume. My little brother Tony was Superman with a red cape and mask that covered only his eyes. I know that she spent many hours with her sewing machine making these costumes not only because it was Halloween but because she really loved us. I remember running around our yard singing and humming the Batman theme pretending to have the strengths and superpowers of the Caped Crusader.

My mom used her sewing abilities many times throughout our childhood to do whatever she could to make sure that her five children were clothed well. In the early 70s when I was in seventh grade, tie-dyed clothing was fashionable. It was after the end of the Vietnam War and tie-dyed clothing was a fad that came from hippies and their representation of peace and love. I had seen in a magazine someone wearing a pair of tie-dyed pants with large bell bottoms and a matching vest. My mom told me that she could make that outfit for me and proceeded to work hard at her sewing machine. I was so excited to wear it when she was finished and decided that it would be fashionable and cool to wear to school. Unfortunately to my dismay, the school dress code prohibited tie-dye clothes and I was sent home that day by the school principal. I was slightly embarrassed, but my mom was angry. She called the school and complained that she had spent many hours making this outfit and didn't understand why it was prohibited. She was a bit timid at times but when it came to standing up for her kids she would be very vocal.

Dad was the disciplinarian of our family and we were always fearful when we were in trouble that my mother would say, "Wait till your father gets home". Unfortunately, this always put him in an unfavorable light with us. Often instead of looking forward to him coming home and being able to happily spend the limited time we had with him, we kept our distance because he was the authority that we had to deal with. I think that this situation resulted from my affectionate mother being very passive about punishment. It was obvious that my parents had different personalities and showed their love in different ways. We gravitated towards my mother because she was around us more often and was much softer and more openly affectionate with us. I respected and loved my father but had difficulty relating to him because he kept so many of his feelings inside, including what he experienced in the military and during his childhood.

My dad's grandparents and parents were immigrants from Syria and had settled in New Kensington, PA because of job opportunities with Alcoa Aluminum. My grandfather, Jacob Alexander Jacob, worked as a laborer, and my grandmother, Fefe, was a homemaker for their family of six children. They spoke Arabic to each other and learned English here in the United States. My father and his siblings all were raised speaking English. I was told that my grandfather was very strict, also. My father left the house at the age of 15 to join the Marines by forging his father's signature. It was in the 1940s and he was stationed in China for several years. I was always impressed to see his Marines jacket with the scripted Chinese label that he had brought back from his tour of duty. He never really spoke much about his time there but I always imagined that it would have been very difficult for a teenager to be in the military so far away from his home and family. I think that this time in the military as a boy stripped him of his teenage years and shaped him into the stern and serious father that we knew.

When he returned home he went back to high school to get his degree and competed in amateur boxing. He had great ambition and decided to pursue a college degree at the University of Miami in Florida. After earning his bachelor's degree in physical education, he became interested in becoming a physical therapist and entered a program at the University of Pennsylvania in Philadelphia. I admired his strong work ethic that propelled him to continue his education. He instilled this value in me. His Syrian immigrant parents had never been formally educated in the United States and he was the first of his siblings to pursue college and a professional career.

It was during his schooling in Miami that he met his future bride and my mother Jacqueline Larocque. My mom was more extroverted than my father and was from a much different upbringing. Her French-Canadian father, Roger, was a truck driver for Mobil gas and her mother, Agnes, was a registered nurse who worked in the local Gardner hospital. Mom was a licensed practical nurse and was working at a health center on campus at the University of Miami. It was fate that they both lived in the same apartment complex and met in passing. They fell in love and when my father decided to continue his schooling in Philadelphia, he asked my mom to come along with him. Eventually they got married and moved back to New Kensington where my father started his career and my mother began to raise our family. As a physical therapist my dad worked very hard at his profession but often his work kept him from spending time with our family and getting to know us better. He worked a full-time job during the day, a part-time job three evenings a week along with Saturday mornings, and was a commissioned officer in the Army Reserves which required him to spend at least one weekend per month away from us. This meant that I would typically only see him later in the evenings and on three Sundays per month. I feel that his dedication to his work created a strain on his marriage and hindered his relationship with his children.

Some of my fondest memories of my father were when he would take my brother Jeff and I out to jog with him. He would wake us early in the morning before school and take us down to the closest park so that we could run several times around the perimeter. We both hated it at the time because we ran in adverse weather conditions and never enjoyed getting up early. However, despite our outward feelings, I always enjoyed the attention of my father spending time with me and the infrequent touch of his hand on my shoulder. His physical therapy background made him a strong advocate for regular exercise and he always encouraged us to participate in whatever way possible. At an early age he would have us doing 40 push-ups every night before we went to bed. At the time we never really understood why we needed to do push-ups, but we did them because we were told to by him. I guess this was his way of raising us so that we would grow up healthy and conscientious of our physical fitness. I learned the importance of physical exercise from him and it encouraged me to pursue sports and, ultimately, the challenges of wrestling.

My Love of Wrestling

I was a small kid growing up, usually one of the smallest in my classrooms throughout school. I always liked sports and doing well in athletic competition. My parents encouraged me to participate in sports and athletics. I competed on many youth teams and usually did well, but it was my experience in seventh grade when I tried out for the junior high school basketball team that sparked my interest to pursue wrestling.

My best friend at the time and I decided that we would try out for the basketball team together even though we were both quite small in comparison to our peers. We often practiced together behind his house in the alley in preparation for the tryouts and had become pretty good at making layups and outside shots. The tryouts were a two-day process but it was obvious to me that the team had already been picked before the tryouts even began. The coach selected those kids that were the tallest of the bunch despite much lack of athletic ability or coordination. He also selected the kids that had played previously since he was familiar with their abilities. We didn't stand a chance. This was my first exposure to true favoritism in sports, and it made me bitter about the whole tryout process. I realized that this selection was based upon the coach's decision and had nothing to do with my abilities. I decided that I wanted to pursue a sport in which I could be fairly matched against my opponent and making the team would not be based upon anyone's favoritism.

We had a family membership at the New Kensington YMCA and were involved with many activities there. Moe Guin was starting a wrestling program and was looking for kids of all ages who were interested in the sport. I liked that I was able to compete with kids of the same age and weight class as myself and that being small was not a disadvantage in wrestling. My friend since elementary school, Joe Galli, decided to join the program, and like me he was small but competitive. We became wrestling partners throughout high school and always competed with each other. This friendly competition helped both of us to learn that hard work was essential to becoming successful. Later in life, he became the CEO of several Fortune 500 companies throughout his career.

I also loved that wrestling gave me the ability to control my own destiny because in selecting a team, there is no question about who is the starter for each weight class. You wrestle against your opponent and at the end of the regular time periods, there is a winner and a loser. There is no question about who will be chosen because if you win the match, then you are the starter. No coach favoritism or concerns about height, weight or physical stature. It was perfect for me.

Wrestling gave me the opportunity to excel in a sport and develop character over the many years that I competed. In high school, I was coached by Chad Hanna who taught our team discipline and hard work. He was not an extremely-skilled clinician but he made sure that we were in excellent condition and helped us to get the most out of ourselves. I mention this because I honestly feel that the hard work and discipline that I learned through wrestling helped me to deal with my disability later in life and recognize that no matter what obstacles were laid in front of me, I could overcome them with hard work. Chad was a no-nonsense coach who expected his wrestlers to work hard and in return he would be there to support us. We all respected him for this and to this day he remains a friend. He has supported me throughout my life dealing with a disability.

In high school I was fortunate to win numerous tournaments and developed a reputation as a "pinner". This meant that I often tried to pin my opponents ending the match as quickly as possible. I was a lanky wrestler in my lightweight class and had the advantage of having long arms. This was ideal for using a "cradle" which is a move that locks up your opponent's head and leg together resulting in them not being able to move. I pinned many of my opponents in my high school wrestling career and caught the eye of several college wrestling coaches.

My parents decided to start me in first grade when I was only five years old. My mom later told me that this was because I was ready for school, but I really think it was because she had a house full of kids and getting me started and out of the house was simpler. Unfortunately, this made me a year younger than most of my classmates and often younger than many of my opponents. I began tenth grade, which was the beginning of our high school, at the age of 14. This was a real disadvantage to me because physical maturity is a big factor for young boys in sports. Despite this, I became a member of the varsity team at 15 years old and easily won the section championship along with the Westmoreland County championship. In the regional championships, I lost to a guy that was 18 and much more physically mature than I was. I started my senior year at 16 years old and turned 17 midway through the season. Despite this disadvantage, I was able to again win the section championship, wrestle in the regional championship and qualify for the state tournament. In my first match of the state tournament, I was very nervous having never wrestled at this level and, unfortunately, lost a very close 5-4 match. There were no consolation matches at that time so this was the end of my high school wrestling career.

After graduating from high school in 1976, I was

recruited to wrestle at the University of Pittsburgh, a quite reputable Division I wrestling program and university. Coach Dave Adams must have recognized my ability to be able to wrestle in college and make his team. I started out wrestling at the light weight of 126 pounds and competed with many other exceptional wrestlers that had been also recruited for this team. With much work during my freshman year, I made the varsity squad and wrestled in several dual meets.

In my sophomore year of college, I injured my back during wrestling practice and wasn't able to compete at my previous level. College-level wrestling was very difficult and required much dedication to excel. I became frustrated by this hindrance and had lost focus on my real purpose of being in college, to earn a degree. I was having many problems in my personal life at that time dealing with my parent's divorce and my mother's alcoholism. I recognized that earning a college degree was more important than my wrestling career and decided not to continue beyond my sophomore year. It was a great experience for me and I made many friends along the way but decided that I was not going to make wrestling my career in life and needed to redirect my attention. I had learned much discipline and determination through my coaches and the sport, as well as from family and friends. I didn't know that these values would be called upon later for the greatest wrestling match in my life.

"The Room"

When I first opened my eyes, I was heavily medicated and barely recognized that I was in a small room in the Intensive Care Unit. I could see while lying flat on my back that there was light from a window directly behind my head and that the entry door and a glass window were at my feet. The nursing station was directly across from my room and I could hear their voices and activity. This room was to become my home for the next six weeks as I struggled with the trauma that my body had encountered and the start of recovery.

I didn't know how long I had been unconscious or what they had done to me, and I was unable to speak because I was intubated. I remember seeing my father's grieved face as he tried to explain that there was internal bleeding in my neck and that I needed to immediately go back into surgery to close up "the bleeder" that had caused my neck to swell with blood. The bone chip that was initially placed into my cervical column to create stability at the point of the break had slipped, making the first surgery unsuccessful. It was determined that this time, rather than going in through the rear of my neck, they would go in through the front and immobilize the cervical fourth and fifth vertebrae with a metal rod. This operation was intended to relieve direct pressure on the spinal cord but also to realign my spinal column at the area of the break. When I woke again I realized that the tube inserted through my mouth into my throat made it so I was still unable to speak, so I began to make a puckering noise with my lips whenever I wanted to get someone's attention. I must have sounded strange making unintelligible noises while lying there unable to move.

I had been placed in a Stryker bed that was designed to be able to flip my immobilized body from front to back to relieve pressure points. If I were to continue to lay flat on my back without relieving pressure points at the back of my head, shoulder blades, tailbone and heels, the blood circulation would be cut off at these points and create pressure sores. Pressure sores can be dangerous to your skin because without proper care they will continue to get larger and can become infected, leading to many other problems. The nursing staff would place a bracing on top of my body that would strap me down tightly and then flip my bed over so that I was off of my back and facing the floor. I was frightened every time they flipped me because I felt so helpless not being able to move and having no control of my body. I always felt as if I was going to fall onto the floor. I felt fear the entire time that I faced downward. I guess I was fortunate that throughout this time I was highly-medicated and not very cognizant of what was happening. Every day was confusing because I never really knew what my status was and what my future would be.

It was eventually decided that it would be best for me to be fitted into a cervical halo cast in order to immobilize my neck completely and prevent any further damage to my spinal column rather than return to the Stryker bed. This halo cast looked exactly like it sounds. A metal halo was placed around my skull, slightly above my eyebrows, and was screwed into my skull in four locations, one screw in each temple area and two in the back of my head. This halo was attached to a jacket cast that was fitted around my chest and upper body. The halo and jacket were connected by metal rods that kept my spinal column aligned straightly and immobilized. This contraption was brutal because the pins that were screwed into my head continued to bleed and when the blood dried it became very itchy and uncomfortable. I was unable to scratch the itch and the feeling of the dried blood was horrible. The jacket cast was lined with a lambswool material which provided a soft padding designed to prevent pressure sores on my skin and make the fit more secure. It seemed like a rather archaic way to deal with a broken neck. Even though it was not pretty, it was effective.

I would often try to ask my mother if she would scratch my head for me because of the intense itch from the dried blood. I would make odd sounds to her that she would try to interpret, eventually directing her to my needs. The nurses were unable to truly clean the blood from the back of my head because I was required to lay on my back and they could not reach the rear pinholes. In my vanity to keep my hair prior to surgery, I never imagined that the doctors would eventually need to screw into the back of my head. A shaved head would have been a much cleaner surface instead of having hair matted with blood. Wow, what we do in the name of vanity!

I often faded in and out of consciousness throughout the first few weeks. I recall thinking about Thanksgiving and the joy of eating regular food again. It was that time of year and I often heard the nursing staff talking about their preparation for the holiday. I do not have much recollection of my twentieth birthday on December 23, because it was like every other day in the hospital. Birthdays were supposed to be special days to celebrate advancing another year in life. This birthday was quite different from those in the past and at the time I wished it had never come.

When I was awake, I tried to move my hands and feet but always seemed to be unsuccessful. My efforts made me become more depressed. As a dedicated athlete in my youth, I was able to accomplish most of what I strived for by focusing on the task at hand and working extremely hard to accomplish it. This was a whole new animal. I was unable to accomplish what I desired even though I told myself that I could and should be able to overcome this situation. I figured that I was not like the others with disabilities who I had seen in wheelchairs. My father had a close friend who was also his accountant, Bill Coleman, who was confined to a manual wheelchair. I had known him for many years. Bill had incurred a spinal cord injury when he was a young boy and still lived with his disability many years later. He was my first real exposure to a person with a disability, coincidentally a very similar type of injury to mine. I remember helping my father to carry Bill up and down a flight of steps into our home whenever he would visit. I never minded helping Bill into our house because he was friendly and was my father's friend. I never imagined that I would eventually deal with even worse physical limitations than he had.

Many of my friends would come to visit me, and I always felt a bit of embarrassment having them see me in this incapacitated condition. I was a meticulous dresser and had a lot of pride in the way that I presented myself and my physical presence. I couldn't see my body lying flat on my back but I knew that I must look quite different with my halo cast around my head, breathing tube down my throat and IVs in my arms. I didn't want my friends to see me this way. Looking back at that time it was crazy of me to have any concerns about my appearance. I am sure that my friends and family who visited only wanted me to get better and didn't care about how I looked.

After my second surgery, I began to have more trouble breathing on my own because of the paralysis and congestion in my lungs. It was determined that I would need to have a tracheotomy so that my breathing could be controlled with a ventilator. This involved making a small slice into the front of my throat and inserting a tube through to provide oxygen without any constrictions. This procedure was successful in assisting me to breathe but left me with no ability to speak. I often would lie awake at night and listen to the sound of the ventilator as it would swoosh up and down, pushing air into my lungs. I would count the seconds between each stage of the ventilator's push and was often fearful that if it stopped, I would not be able to breathe, and the nursing staff would never know until it was too late. I didn't want to die because I expected to soon return to my promising young life. I felt that I had so much to live for.

I was very fortunate to have my close friend BJ Rayburg available to me during this traumatic time in my life. He was a guy from my hometown who I had gotten to know well a few years before, and we hung out together a lot. We worked together one summer as youth placement counselors for a county program that was developed to assist young kids with taking on job responsibilities at local job sites. We were required to drive into Greensburg, the local county capital, every week and would share rides. It was, at times, lots of fun having the freedom to set our own schedules and make decent money throughout the summer. The program typically hired students who were in college and off for the summer. This fit perfectly for BJ and me because it gave us an opportunity to make money, drive around the county and be free to be outside most of the time enjoying the summer weather. We were also bartenders together at the local country club when I turned 18 years old. Although neither of us had any experience as bartenders, we were hired and spent most of the time working on weekends for large events like weddings and parties. It was a recipe for disaster, having two 18-year-old guys running the bar without much supervision, because we found that it was very easy to pour drinks for the patrons and also sip upon others for ourselves. It made for a very interesting summer for us.

We were both attending Penn State New Kensington as students for the fall term of 1978 when my injury occurred. I had gotten to know his parents during this time because I spent a lot of time at his house. He had a very close-knit family. They often invited me over for dinner because they knew that my family life was broken, and I didn't have any home-cooked meals. BJ always looked up to me because he envied my success in sports and girls' attraction to me. I had always considered BJ a good friend but realized after my accident how loyal he really was. He spent many days sitting in my room while I was in intensive care and visited me daily during my stay at the rehabilitation hospital. Even though my exterior appearance and physical abilities had changed, he stayed by my side when times were the worst. We often cried together wishing for things to get better and talking about fun times in the past. I remember him telling me that he wished that he could take on some of my paralysis to help me and we could deal with this situation together. Friends like BJ are hard to find, and I have always considered myself fortunate to have him in my life.

In the summer just prior to my accident, I had been dating a girl named Patty Sleppy. She was 18 years old and was from my hometown of New Kensington. I remember first seeing her at a high school graduation party in the spring and became interested in her because she had a sense of maturity and culture that I hadn't found in other girls that I had dated. I was shy about approaching her because I was intrigued by her reputation as a top student in her graduating class and a previous winner of the local Junior Miss pageant. She was a girl with a good reputation and I liked that about her. Why? I don't know, I guess that I wanted to be around someone who was smarter than me and could enrich my experiences. She had lived in Australia for a few years with her family while her father worked as an engineer with Alcoa Aluminum. She played the piano, sang opera and was a gymnast. She was different than any girl I had known before and I enjoyed her company. We dated throughout the summer of 1978. I eventually realized that we were very different, and I began to lose interest in her. Our relationship never developed into a sexual encounter even though the opportunity existed. I never wanted to go that far with her because I knew that I liked her very much but was not in love with her. I guess that I respected her too much and didn't want to ever feel that I had used her.

She had entered college at Ohio University in the fall to pursue her desire of becoming a veterinarian. The school was a three-hour drive from New Kensington and we stopped dating at the start of the fall because of the distance and, truthfully, because I just didn't have enough interest anymore. When she heard about my accident, she traveled back to the hospital to see me. I pretended to sleep while she was there and did not talk with her. I remember trying to ignore her and wishing that she would go away. In reality, I was embarrassed to have her see me in this fragile condition because when we dated I was very physically active and healthy. I wanted her to remember me as that person and not as this newly-incapacitated guy who, in my opinion, could not be attractive to anyone. It was a very cold way to treat a good friend who cared very much about me. Unfortunately, I was only thinking about myself at the time and was not concerned about other people's feelings. As she sat by my bedside I could hear her speaking with my mother.

It seemed that they talked forever and I could hear the sadness in her voice. Patty was concerned and she wanted to help however she could, but sadly I only wished for her to leave. I pushed her away from me emotionally as I began to do with many of the friends who would come in to see me.

I guess this was the start of me no longer seeing myself as a good-looking, healthy male but instead as a disabled guy who may never be attractive to anyone. It was very hard to deal with this new perception of myself, and I did not want to involve others. Dealing with a life-changing incident, I became very insecure about my self-image and it took many years for me to regain my confidence to deal with life as it is. In later years, I would reconnect with Patty over the phone and apologize to her for my actions. I had read the obituary of her father in our local paper and realized that she would be coming back into town for the funeral. I guessed that she would be staying at her parents' home and called that number hoping to catch her while she was there. We talked about our families, the summer that we had spent together, our new lives and the effects of my accident. I am very happy that I was able to do that because it hurt me for a long time knowing that I could have been so cold to a friend who just wanted to show that she cared.

I feel guilty now that I was not grateful for the people around me at that time who cared deeply for the pain and suffering that I was going through, but I was depressed. I recall it being near Christmas time and my friends BJ, Katie Armstrong and Cindy Hardy bought me an electric razor to use on my often hairy face. It was actually a great gift because I had previously used a blade razor which would be very awkward for me to use going forward. However, I didn't want to imagine that I would continue to live in this state of paralysis, with no use of my legs, arms and hands forever. If I accepted that I would not be able to use my blade razor anymore, then I was accepting that I wouldn't be able to regain my mobility and return to my previous self. I decided to let my mother try the electric razor on me with much reservation and quickly concluded that I hated it. It was actually a great shave, but I didn't want to accept any changes from my former lifestyle. I never thanked them for the Christmas gift and instead directed my anger towards them rather than being thankful for their efforts to make me happy. I recognize now how mean it was of me, but at the time my spirit had been broken and I was taking it out on the people around me.

My father would come to the hospital every night after work to visit and sit next to my bed. We had a strained relationship at that time because he and my mother had recently divorced and he had a very difficult time adjusting to her leaving. We were all dealing with a lot. I had been 18 and in my freshman year of college when they separated and decided to divorce.

My mother was at my bedside every day from the start of the morning till the early evening, spending many hours with me in that room. My mother and father were not speaking to each other. It was awkward to have them together in the same room, so when one would come in the other would leave. It was heartbreaking to have them separated when I needed them both so badly.

I enjoyed the sensation of my mother gently scratching the top of my head with her nails because it was the only thing I had that was pleasurable. I couldn't feel anything below my shoulders and this loss of sensation was difficult to adjust to. I didn't expect my mother to be there through the night but sometimes wished that she would. It was comforting to have her there because in my completely dependent state I was scared to be left alone and sometimes would wake up in the middle of the night and be fearful because no one was there. Being alone, completely paralyzed, without the ability to breathe on my own was petrifying. Part of me wished my ventilator would stop working and this would all be over, that I would not need to deal with this situation anymore. The other part of me wanted to fight back and keep living with hope that I would recover and be able to live a normal life again.

My time in the room became more complicated as I spent more time flat on my back with no movement. Inactivity of my body allowed for mucus to accumulate in my lungs and I could hear it with every breath. The only way to remove this was to have a nurse insert a very thin suction tube up into my nostril and down my windpipe into my lungs. It was awful to have that damn tube shoved into my head. Instead of removing the mucus that was gurgling around inside my lungs, the suction would remove the oxygen that remained and leave me feeling like I had suffocated. When the tube was removed I would sometimes feel that I was blacking out. I knew that the only way to begin to breathe clearly again was to suction this mucus out, but I feared the adverse effect of the oxygen being removed from my lungs. I couldn't even move to signal to the nurse when to stop and I began to fear every time they began to prepare the suction tube. Many times I would close my eyes and feel the tube as it was inserted into my nostril just counting inside my head the amount of time it took until it was removed. I tried to mentally remove myself from the situation, picturing myself in a better place and time. I often thought that I would die from lack of oxygen and began to accept that this would be my fate.

In order to keep the mucus from settling in my lungs the staff decided that it was necessary to roll me onto my side to change my positioning. I really had no choice in the matter because I was completely incapacitated and had no way to express my thoughts about any type of treatment. I was afraid that when they began to roll me on my side that the mucus flux would dislodge and cut off my ability to breathe. Eventually, it happened. During a late evening, I had a life-changing experience that I remember clearly to this day because it made such an impact on my life to come. As I was rolled onto my side, the mucus in my lungs dislodged and completely blocked my ability to breathe. My mother was in the room along with the nursing staff as I struggled to get oxygen into my lungs. The pain had become very intense and I realized that this is what it must feel like to be drowning. I first remember hearing someone calling my name "Brian" loudly but quickly the calls became faint as I drifted away and eventually I couldn't hear anything. Suddenly, the intense pain just stopped, and I was relieved to no longer feel anything. All of the pain in my neck, the hurt throughout my head and the weight in my chest was gone. This was the first time since I had had my accident that I actually felt good. Not just good but great! There was no longer any noise from the ventilator or screaming voices or calls from the overhead system, and my body felt weightless. I could feel my whole body begin to float up off of the bed and settle above the room in the small corner to the right of the head of the bed. As I was no longer in my body, I could see myself laying on the hospital bed with several people hovering over top of me trying to resuscitate me. It was very strange because I could see them frantically trying to revive me, and I remember thinking that I must be dead. It was amazing that I was viewing the whole scenario while floating above everything that was happening below. I remember seeing my mother, and I felt bad because I knew that she was very scared and I didn't want her to be worried about me anymore. I recall that I was happy to be out of that useless body and free from the pain. In a state of euphoria I began to drift towards a bright light that seemed to be drawing me closer and closer. I was not afraid to go because I realized how beautiful it would be and knew all of my problems would be gone.

Then I began to faintly hear my name being called again. It became louder and more frequent. "Brian, Brian, Brian." I opened my eyes and there I was, back in my body again, sucking for air and seeing the faces of people over top of me. I really didn't want to go back, but I guess God decided that it just wasn't my time yet. This out-of-body experience made me realize that God was with me and that there was a much greater place for me eventually, but not just yet. On that day, it just wasn't my time.

I have drawn upon this experience many times when I feel low and wish for a different outcome to my life. The feeling of complete relaxation and loss of all pain is a feeling that must only come in heaven. I realize that this story may be hard to believe for many people, but to me it is as real as the day is long. I had been raised in a Catholic family but had never been the type of Christian that would reveal my faith and innermost feelings to others regarding religion. It was never in my personality to be extroverted and discuss my faith with anyone –– people that I don't know or family members. I relate this story only because it has shaped my life and has given me a much stronger belief in my faith and future life to come. I no longer fear death because I know that when it does come I will be ready for the feeling of euphoria that I experienced in the ICU that day. My only reluctance is to leave my family, but I recognize that someday they will join me in a whole new world. I imagine that it will be a world where I can run, be unencumbered by splints, binders and straps, and once again be independent and able to feel the many pleasures that I have missed for so long.

After the tracheotomy was performed on me, the breathing tubes were taken out of my nose, giving me easier access to oxygen through the ventilator. Also, I regained the ability to use my mouth for communication. However, it was difficult because I could only speak in sync with the downward stroke of the ventilator which pushed air into my lungs and allowed me to exhale through my mouth. I was very concerned that I needed to be assisted with breathing through a machine. I often wondered as I lay in my room if I would need to have this with me for the rest of my life.

Starting Rehabilitation

It was on a frigid cold day after nearly two months in intensive care that I was transferred to the Harmarville Rehabilitation Center located on the outskirts of Pittsburgh, PA. My condition had stabilized enough that the physicians hoped that I would be able to participate in the required minimum of three hours of therapy per day. I really wasn't ready for this stage of intensive rehabilitation, but my father had previously directed the physical therapy department at this rehabilitation center and spoke directly with the Medical Director to assist with getting my admission approved. He felt that the sooner I got out of the intensive care unit and into a rehabilitation setting, the more beneficial it would be for my recovery.

I remember the fear of leaving the hospital room that I hated but had come to feel safe in, but it was time for me to go. When the exterior doors opened, I could feel the cold air on my face and in my lungs. At that moment, fresh air had never smelled so good but seemed so foreign. It was the start of me going back out into the unsheltered world that had left me paralyzed and begin dealing with life from a whole different perspective. I had been a carefree teenager with many hopes and aspirations before the day of the accident. Now my outlook on life was completely changed. I had never worried about having other people take care of me and always felt very fortunate despite many of the family issues that I had dealt with. I wondered what it would be like having a life depending upon other people all the time and dealing with the loneliness of never having a spouse to love and to love me. Would I be able to deal with these emotions? Would I ever be happy again?

I had not felt the winter air yet that season because when I went into the hospital in mid-November it had not been very cold. Now it was the start of January in Southwestern Pennsylvania, though. The ambulance staff wrapped me in blankets that showed only a very small part of my face because they were so fearful of me being exposed to the low temperature. My mother stood by the side of the gurney and told me that it was only 6°F and that they were taking every precaution available to keep me warm. At that time, I was vulnerable to any type of illness that could result in pneumonia because my system was too weak to battle back.

The drive to the rehabilitation center took only about 20 minutes. I wondered what was in store for me. My dad had told me that I needed to start rehabilitation, but I really had no idea what that involved. I remembered visiting my father at work when I was a young boy and was intrigued by the rehabilitation facility, but I had been a bit apprehensive about dealing with patients who had some type of physical limitation or disability. I was fortunate to have a recognized and reputable rehabilitation center located close to my home. My father knew many of the administrators and physicians because he had worked as the Director of Physical Therapy for this organization for many years when I was a youngster. I think that it made the admission and transition into this facility a bit smoother because many of the staff members had heard about my accident and were very gracious in accommodating me because of their relationships with my dad.

I was still completely paralyzed with no movement in my arms or legs and the halo cast affixed around my head and trunk. My breathing had been stabilized, though. I was extremely nervous to arrive at this facility for many reasons that included the uncertainty of what rehabilitation could do for me and how much I could return to my earlier self. I could feel the shaking of the ambulance and could hear the hum of the tires on the cold asphalt roads as we headed on our trip. I tried to divert my attention away from thinking about the future because it was so uncertain and scary to me. I would often imagine myself as that athletic person that had an envious physique and confidence to get the attention of many girls. I was now 20 years old and the spinal cord injury had left me with no sensation from my shoulders down, complete loss of bowel and bladder control and lack of sexual function. The latter was very concerning to a young male who couldn't imagine what life would be like without the ability to control an erection. Funny that at that time the paralysis took a backseat to the ever-concerning thought that I would never be able to participate in sexual intercourse again. I was hopeful and prayed that rehabilitation would be the answer to my multiple problems, reversing the paralysis and making everything normal like it was before.

Within a few days of arriving, I had a thorough evaluation with Dr. Gilbert Brenes, a physician who specialized in physical medicine. His specialty was dealing with the many aftereffects of spinal cord injury or trauma. Dr. Brenes was fairly new to the rehabilitation center and had been working on the spinal cord unit for only a few years. He was young and had a foreign accent that made understanding him very difficult. He was small in stature with a Napoleon complex. He would march into the room and his team of support staff would follow closely behind him waiting for his indiscernible orders. Regardless, there was much respect amongst the staff for Dr. Brenes because he was extremely dedicated to his patients and expected his staff to be the same.

Dr. Brenes had scheduled to meet with my parents and me to discuss my condition. As I lay on the gurney in my halo cast looking at the ceiling, he began to describe to me my parents the specifics of a spinal cord injury and its effects. He used the analogy of a banana in its skin being squeezed and although the inside of the banana maintains its content, the soft fruit has been crushed and never returns to its previous form. I could see my mom and dad sitting near me in this small treatment room, but I was unable to see their faces because of my supine position. It was probably for the best that I was unable to see their expressions as Dr. Brenes described to us the severity of my injury. He told us that I had incurred a break in my spinal cord between the fourth and fifth cervical segments. My injury would mean permanent paralysis that included all of my body except above my shoulders. I think that my parents knew what this report was going to be because they seemed to be less shocked by this diagnosis than I was. I became very angry to think that this young doctor could tell me that I had lost movement and sensation of my body, control of my bodily functions and the inability to ever father a child. How could he know that this was my future? Only months ago I was a young man with a bright future ahead of me. His words seemed so cold and I felt as though I was in the middle of a bad dream waiting for someone to wake me up and end this nightmare.

I questioned his ability to make this diagnosis about me. His foreign accent made it difficult for me to understand what he was saying at times and in some warped way made it easier for me to distance myself from the conversation going on around me. This was not the news that I was expecting to hear when my father told me that I needed to go to rehabilitation. I thought that coming here would be the solution to my problems and that I would be able to work hard and fix this bad situation. I had always thought that hard work and dedication would be the solution to any problem as had been instilled in me through my many years of wrestling.

Accepting Quadriplegia

Every day during my six-month stay at the Harmarville Rehabilitation Center was a day closer to me accepting that I now had limitations that would be permanent in my life. I was admitted at the start of January and would not be discharged until late June 1979. There were many other young patients like myself who had sustained similar injuries and were trying to work their way through this maze of uncertainty that surrounded us and our futures. I was assigned to a room with four beds and a shared bathroom. My roommates were all young men who had spinal cord injuries like mine but had different levels of mobility. The bed next to mine was occupied by Gary who was in a car accident resulting in quadriplegia and across the room were two others who were paraplegics. The difference is that a quadriplegic is a person who has all four extremities affected and a paraplegic has only the legs affected, not the arms.

I was strangely envious of my roommates that had the use of their arms and were able to dress themselves, transfer out of bed, move around easily in their wheelchairs and maintain a level of independence. Hard to believe that anyone could actually be envious of a paraplegic, but I guess you always wish that you could have what you don't. Paraplegics have many difficult issues that they need to deal with throughout life and by no means should be envied by anyone. Except maybe quadriplegics? I often thought that high-level quadriplegics like myself were at the bottom of the totem pole in the rehab center. We were the ones that could do the least and depended on nursing staff to assist us daily.

It was necessary for the therapy staff to start acclimating me to sitting up again because I had been lying on my back in the hospital during those first two months. If I was raised into a sitting position too quickly without having time to acclimate, I would begin to blackout. They would lay me on a table that could be tilted incrementally upward and every day the degree of tilting would be increased. I dreaded these daily sessions because I had blacked out many times and often gotten nauseous during this process. I knew that it was going to be scary and uncomfortable but also knew that it was necessary so that I could get used to sitting up straight again. The initial goal was to be able to get into a seated position so that I could then be seated in a wheelchair. After being seated in a wheelchair, the next goal would be to build up what was called your "seating tolerance". This is the amount of time that you are able to stay in a seated position without becoming too tired and also being able to strengthen the skin under your normal sitting area. Rehabilitation is a slow and gradual process that hopefully results in the patient reaching their highest level of independence possible.

During one of the many daily sessions on this tilt table as I lay flat on my back and unable to see around me, I heard the sound of an electric wheelchair motoring up next to me. A man with a voice that made him sound slightly older than me introduced himself as Terry. He began to explain to me that he also had suffered a spinal cord injury several years ago by a freak accident. He told me that he was driving his car in Canada and suddenly a large moose started to cross the highway in front of his car. His car hit the moose and it flew up into the air and landed on the roof. The weight of this large animal crushed the roof down on to him and broke his neck in a similar location to where my spinal cord injury had occurred. After much rehabilitation and going back to school, he had become a counselor and was now working and seemed to be living a fulfilled life. How bizarre was it that he had a spinal cord injury from a moose landing on his head? This was a story that you had to hear from someone who had experienced it in order to believe it! I laid there wondering what he looked like and imagined that he would not need his electric wheelchair much longer. I figured that if his injury had happened several years ago then he could be much nearer to walking again. It wasn't until several months later that I met Terry again and this time could see what he looked like. I was surprised to see that he was nothing like I had initially imagined. I thought that he would be somebody near ready to stand up with a fully-developed body. Instead, he was a young man of small stature with very small shoulder muscles that had atrophied from paralysis and wrist splints that supported hands that had contracted from limited use. It was probably better that I had not been able to see him initially as I lay on that table because it would have scared the hell out of me to think that this is what I would probably end up looking like.

During my first few months in rehab all I wanted to do was lie in bed with a pillow over my head hoping that the world would forget about me. I often felt cold; laying in bed under the covers with a pillow over my head was warming and allowed me to disengage from the real world around me. I found it very comforting to not be able to see anyone and pretend that they could not see me. Unfortunately, this wasn't the case because the rehabilitation staff knew that I needed to start getting into a daily routine where I would get up out of bed and be seated in my wheelchair. I hated waking up every morning to the realization that I was paralyzed. These nurses and therapy staff had a job to do, but most days I just didn't want to deal with them. I would have preferred that they leave me alone and let me die.

My wheelchair! How dare they assign a wheelchair to me. I wanted to believe that I would eventually be able to walk again and simply get out of this place. I hated even looking at that damn wheelchair because to me it was a sign of weakness and the disability that I was having such a hard time accepting. The nurses would come into our room after 6 a.m. and start the daily routine of getting me dressed and ready to be transferred to sitting in my wheelchair. My halo cast made it difficult to transfer me because it was so bulky and made my trunk top-heavy. Sitting at about a 45° angle, I would be transferred down to the physical therapy gym where they would start stretching exercises to keep the muscles and tendons in my arms and legs from contracting. After this session came lunch time.I was slowly starting to eat regular food again. In the afternoon, I was scheduled for another therapy session with an occupational therapist who would work more specifically with my hands and try to maximize the minimal return that I was starting to get in my right shoulder. Just maintaining a simple daily routine like this would typically wipe me out for the day, and I often was too tired to eat dinner before lying back down in bed.

There was one particular nurse, Charlotte McDermott, who worked closely with Dr. Brenes. She was assigned to the spinal cord unit and was very knowledgeable about dealing with spinal cord patients and our rehabilitation. She worked the day shift and supervised the unit, making sure that all of us patients followed our prescribed treatment plan. She was short and slightly heavy with an attractive face. When I first met her I really disliked her because she was the one who would direct other nurses and aides on the unit and would force me to get out of bed in the morning to begin my rehabilitation treatment plan. She had a loud voice and was not afraid to let it be known when she was in charge. I could hear her voice carrying throughout the unit, directing all of the patients to get up and start getting ready for the day ahead. Starting the day was always agonizing for me because I often felt that this was a life that I could no longer lead. I guess I directed a lot of my anger towards her because of the role that she was in. Throughout my long stay at Harmarville, I learned that she was a very caring nurse and many of the injured spinal cord patients like myself would go to her for advice. I began to accept her direction and learned how truly knowledgeable she was about spinal cord injuries and their effects on the emotions and lives of many young people. She became a trusted friend to me because I knew she cared about her patients and the lives that we faced in the future.

After three months in my halo cast it was time to have it removed. The x-rays showed that the broken bones in my neck had finally healed. I was anxious to have it taken off because it was very awkward to wear and many times I would get extreme headaches due to the pins that had been screwed into my skull. In order to have this cast removed, I was taken into a treatment room and turned on my stomach on the table. When the cast was removed from my back it was revealed that four large pressure sores had formed due to the excessive amount of time that I had lain on my back while in the hospital. They had not been detected before because the upper body cast could not be removed while my neck was healing and I did not have any skin sensation along my back. I had developed a friendship with a student occupational therapist at the rehabilitation center who was doing a student internship at the time that I arrived. He was in the room when the cast was removed and told me that he had almost fainted when he first viewed these sores because he had never seen anything like them. With this body cast no longer in the way, these sores were able to be healed with skilled nursing care.

I was scheduled every day to receive a variety of services that included physical therapy, occupational therapy, recreational therapy, social work, vocational rehab and psychotherapy. I initially expected that my rehabilitation program would be focused on getting me up out of bed and learning to walk and move about as I used to. Unfortunately, I did not start to gain back any muscle movement or sensation as I had hoped. My treatment plan focused mostly on getting me used to moving around in an electric wheelchair and learning how to teach others to care for me. I was an inpatient at this rehabilitation center for over six months, and with the passing of every month I realized that my future would not be what I had hoped before but would be a life with an extreme physical disability and the many difficulties associated with it. This was very difficult to accept, but I recognized that I had no choice and was going to need to deal with it.

I was initially motivated and accepting of participation in this rehabilitation plan, except for the psychology component. I thought to myself, *Why do I need to see a psychologist? My body was injured, not my mind.* Looking back I guess this was my way of denying that this injury could affect my mind and willpower in any way. My assigned psychologist was a woman who was much older than me who I could not relate to. She began asking me questions about how I felt and tried to get into my thoughts as any good psychologist or counselor would. I couldn't accept that this injury had affected my mindset so I decided to discontinue sessions with her. This was really against the norm of spinal cord patients in rehabilitation, but I guess Dr. Brenes recognized that I wasn't going to speak with her so there was no reason for me to continue with psychotherapy sessions. My mother knew that I could be very hard headed. She encouraged me to participate, but at the time I could not see the benefit of discussing my thoughts and emotions with anyone.

I think that I was a difficult patient who was often obstinate with the nurses, therapists and doctors who were trying their best to help me. As a young man in the prime of his life, I was not ready to accept this disability or months in a facility with many other disabled people. I wanted to be back in college with my friends, going to classes and fraternity parties, drinking beer, meeting girls, just being a regular student and experiencing life. My brother Jeff who was one year older than me continued in his college life at Slippery Rock University. I was so jealous that he could do everything I wanted to do but was now unable to. It wasn't fair of me to begrudge him and my college friends for something that they had. They could not have changed where I was.

Even though I denied that this spinal cord injury had affected my mind, I was only holding back how insecure it really made me feel. One Saturday afternoon, Linda, my former college psychology professor from Penn State New Kensington, came to visit me. I did not know her well, but she was a very caring person and a good listener. We began to talk about how I felt. I remember it being a cold and rainy day; I was sitting next to a large glass door where I could see the overcast surroundings. I was dealing with many physical issues but didn't realize how deeply I had been affected emotionally. We talked about my youngest brother Tony and how seriously he had been affected by my accident. He and I had always been close while growing up; I was the big brother that took care and watched over him. At the time of my accident he was only 14 years old and had been living at home with only my father and me (when I was home from college). We were often together without our parents because of my mother's alcoholism and my father's devotion to work. I cared deeply about Tony and knew that my accident had changed his life dramatically, as it had mine.

As a young teenager he should have been more closely supervised and given the direction that all teenagers need. He had started to hang around with a group of mischievous neighborhood boys and began to experiment with marijuana. With me being gone and out of the house, nobody was there to watch over him. While in the rehabilitation hospital I was told a story about how Tony had been picked on by some of the older boys in our neighborhood and no one was there to help him. This affected me very deeply because it made me feel so helpless. My little brother whom I'd looked after as we grew up, no longer had me to be there for him. As I told the story to Linda, I cried harder than I had cried in a long time and couldn't stop. My tears were not tears for me but tears for my little brother that I felt I had abandoned when he needed me the most. Linda left me that day and never came back because I think that my grief was much greater than she ever expected to hear and it hurt her too much to listen. That day made me realize emotionally and psychologically I had been greatly affected by my spinal cord injury and it had affected my family and friends who cared very much about me.

Starting Life Again

At the time of my discharge from the rehabilitation center in July 1979, we had to decide where I would live. My father realized that it would be unrealistic for me to move back into our home with him for several reasons. First, our house on Edward Street had numerous levels and was not wheelchair accessible. Secondly, he was working several jobs and would not be able to give up his employment to stay with me. My parents debated about what to do with me due to these circumstances. My father had talked about placing me in a nursing home so that I would be able to receive care at all times. My mother was vehemently against this. She was not willing to place me in this type of setting because she was afraid that I would not receive proper care. I was scared that this might be my only option and cried to my mother to not put me in a nursing home. She told me, "There's no way that I will ever let you live there as long as I'm alive."

It was decided that my father would assist us financially as long as I continued to pursue my education, and I would live with my mother and sister. Since the divorce, they had been living in an apartment that had numerous steps outside and several more inside. They found a reasonably priced, two-bedroom apartment in a neighboring town called Monroeville that could accommodate a wheelchair, and we started making arrangements to move in. I will always be thankful to my mom for her willingness to take on the responsibility of my nursing care and assist me in my return to school. It was obvious that she loved me and would do everything she could, but I was now a twenty-year-old young man forced to live with her because of my circumstances. I had not been living with her for several years due to her alcoholism and divorce from my father, yet here I was now totally physically dependent upon her and my sister, Amy. My mom started working a night shift job on the weekends and Amy would stay with me until the morning when Mom came home. We were living off the wages that my mom earned and the divorce settlement from my father. It was an awkward arrangement, but it allowed me to continue my education and provided me with a semi-normal life.

Our place was situated on the ground floor of an apartment complex, so I had easy access inside through a sliding glass door in the back. The landlord was willing to cut the asphalt curb so that I could roll onto the back patio easily. It seemed like a semi-ideal set up because the rent was reasonable. Besides, we really didn't have many other choices. This apartment provided me with my first real experience of what it was like to live with a disability in a non-institutional setting. When you are a patient in a rehabilitation center, you live in a bubble because everything is accommodating to a wheelchair and you are always surrounded by knowledgeable staff. This was quite different and I started to look at the world from a whole new perspective. Are the doors and hallways wide enough? Can I get into the bathroom? Can I adequately fit under the tabletop? Are the light switches low enough for me to reach? Can I fit my wheelchair and electric bed into the same room? It quickly became obvious to me that this was real life and it wasn't going to be easy.

My mom had met her boyfriend, Paul VanRyn, when she joined Alcoholics Anonymous. We were both very fortunate to have him in our lives at this time. He had gone through his own divorce and lived a very simple life. He cared very much for my mother and was always willing to assist her with my care.

Transportation was difficult because in 1979 there was limited availability of accessible vans. My mom owned a two-door sedan with doors that opened wide enough so that she and Paul could lift me into the front seat. I had lost considerable weight during my rehabilitation stay and only weighed about 135 pounds. This was much lighter than the 170 pounds that I had carried prior to my accident. We learned to use a sliding board that could be propped under my leg and allowed me to slide into the car seat without them having to actually lift all of my body weight. This transfer technique is commonly used with paralyzed people. Once inside the front passenger seat, I would be belted in and my manual wheelchair would be folded up and placed in either the back seat or the trunk. This got me from Point A to Point B, but it was very awkward and difficult. Transferring into the car and then out of the car upon arrival and then doing the inverse to go home was very tiring.

Another problem with this is that it meant that I always had to have two people with me any time that I traveled in a car. In addition, it required that I use a manual wheelchair that could be folded, but then I would not have the ability to move about on my own because I did not have use of my arms to propel a wheelchair. It was frustrating to have to sit in one place and not have the ability to turn around and see my environment. My physician had ordered me an electric wheelchair, but it had not yet arrived. Electric wheelchairs at that time were very heavy, bulky and unable to be disassembled or folded to get into a car trunk. I hated the thought of being confined to an electric wheelchair but recognized that it at least gave me some sense of independence. This kind of chair would allow me to move on my own and not have to depend upon someone to always be behind me pushing.

It was fortunate for me that I had several close friends that wanted to do some fundraising so that I would be able to afford the purchase of an accessible van. While I was still in Harmarville, they began to fundraise. They held a spaghetti dinner and also a boxing match. My brother Jeff, Jimmy "Lutso" Ameris and Rick Feroce were on the boxing card and made it very interesting to watch. Some of them had experience with boxing and those who didn't still put up good fights. The profit from these events would eventually be used to assist my father with the purchase of a light-blue Ford cargo van that was converted to be wheelchair accessible.

A 12-inch raised roof along with an electric lift installed on the side made it much easier to get into than transferring into the car. The Pennsylvania office of vocational rehabilitation assisted with the expense of this conversion because I needed it to pursue my continuing education. With this converted van I was able to travel with just one person as a driver and eventually use an electric wheelchair to get around, giving me much more independence. However, it would take a few years before we raised the money to buy this van. When I first was released from the hospital until after I'd been living with my mother and sister for a few years, I had to continue being transferred in and out of vehicles and using ACCESS vans.

My mom was always the caring person who was willing to help someone in need. As she continued to be an active member in the Alcoholics Anonymous program, there were many pigeons (as they were called) who would latch on to her like a drowning man to a lifesaver vest. These fellow members were often looking for anybody that could provide them with a listening ear and a sympathetic heart. At any one time, mom probably had at least four or five pigeons who were under her wing and always in her ear. She was too trusting of people, especially recovering alcoholics who could easily take advantage of her. Prior to my accident she had purchased a very nice, light-green Buick Cutlass. She had received enough money from my father in their divorce settlement that she was able to afford this vehicle. One of her pigeons needed transportation and she offered to lend him her new car. He returned the car as expected but much to her surprise he had made copies of her car keys and returned later to steal the only form of transportation that she and I had. She had insurance, but a large deductible made the purchase of a similar vehicle impossible.

I started back to college in the summer of 1979 at the insistence of my father. He realized the value to me of continuing my education and was very persistent about me starting back. I decided to take a class at the local Community College of Allegheny County campus which was located in the same city as our new apartment. The strange thing was that I was taking classes with no real idea about what my capabilities were and what my new interest in a career would be. I tried to imagine what I could do without the use of my hands, using an electric wheelchair for mobility and not having the capability to drive a car. It was a very scary feeling because I had always seen myself in a role like physical therapist or chiropractor where I would be physically active.

My mother and I made arrangements for transportation to CCAC by contacting the public ACCESS service. This was another whole headache that I had never imagined. ACCESS required wheelchair riders to be ready for pickup up to one hour prior to the scheduled time. For me this meant that we needed to be ready well in advance of the scheduled class, and schedule for a return ride at the end of the anticipated class time. This public service was notorious for being late and sometimes not showing up at all when expected. There were times when I would miss my scheduled class and had to try to make it up, adding to the frustration and difficulty of returning back to college.

Planning is paramount when dealing with a disability. I had to start thinking well in advance about a number of factors in order to accomplish anything in a day's time. For example, what would the weather be like and how would I dress for the day? Yes, this seems like a very simple question that any adult answers, but as a quadriplegic I didn't have the luxury of dressing light and then putting on a jacket if I got too cold or dressing too heavy and simply taking off layers if I got too hot. Simple things suddenly became more difficult and added to the complexity of every day.

My body's thermostat was affected dramatically by the injury. Without being able to sweat from my chest line down, my body had no way of cooling down whenever the temperature got hot. Also, when my body was too cold I was unable to warm up by increasing my activity and being able to shiver. These are typical body thermostat mechanisms that a healthy person uses to increase their body temperature but were not physically possible for me. I first became aware of my temperature sensitivity when I went on a recreational outing with a group of patients while I was an inpatient at the rehab center. We took a bus trip to a local park to go fishing in the early summer. The day was beautiful, sunny with temperatures in the mid-80s. Prior to my spinal cord injury, this would have been an ideal day to sit in the sun and relax. As I sat on the wharf in my wheelchair in the direct sun, I began to heat up and quickly dehydrate. My body was not sweating and was absorbing heat without being able to cool down. I began to get light headed and could feel my heart starting to pump much faster. My breathing was shallow and I knew that I needed to get out of the heat. Eventually, I got back onto the transport bus into air-conditioning and started to feel better.

Controlling my body temperature has become something that I am now very cautious about. Living near

Pittsburgh, Pennsylvania, the weather is often very cold in the winter which makes it uncomfortable for me to stay outside for any long period of time. I needed to learn to dress completely differently in order to keep my body and legs warm. Sitting in a wheelchair in the cold can be a strange thing because I cannot tell how cold my extremities are. I am not aware of the temperature in many parts of my body because I don't have temperature sensation. Both hot and cold temperatures can be extremely discomforting and even dangerous if proper precautions are not taken.

Despite the many obstacles in front of me, I decided that I would continue in school and simply take one day at a time. Without really knowing what my capabilities were and what type of a career I wanted to be in, I realized that the only way I would be able to ever be happy in my life would be to have a productive lifestyle. In order to achieve this I knew that I needed to have a higher education and the willpower to work very hard. In high school I was an above-average student but had never really applied much effort to my grades because I was so focused on being a wrestler. I guess I had always thought that if I was a good enough wrestler I would be able to get into a decent college. During my first two years at the University of Pittsburgh, I had applied the same theory of study that I had done while in high school. Once again, I thought that I could get by without really needing to study much and would still be able to obtain my education. This was unfortunate because in my sophomore year my grades had begun to reflect my lack of effort.

Starting school as a quadriplegic without the ability to write presented a new challenge. To my advantage, I no longer had many of the distractions to studying that I had had as a nondisabled person. In the past it had been easy to be distracted by my wrestling efforts, going out with friends and living a healthy social life. As a quadriplegic, I could now focus all of my attention on my education and study habits. In the coming year I re-registered with Pitt in the College of General Studies. This school was mostly devoted to offering classes in the evening for students who were working during the day or someone like myself who found it more convenient to attend in the later part of the day.

The Dreaded Spasms

As I started back to the University of Pittsburgh, I was still trying to adjust to numerous medications that were prescribed to me for control of involuntary muscle spasms. The spasms were triggered by sensations of pressure to my skin that I could not feel but that my body reacted to. Leaving a warm building and going out into the cold could easily trigger spasms in my back, neck or legs. A simple or sudden touch on my arm or leg could also set off a muscle spasm.

Because of the spasms, I had to strap both of my feet onto the foot pedals of my wheelchair in order to keep them from jumping off and being injured if I was unaware of their location. When your legs are paralyzed and you have no sensation, you learn to rely on your vision to know where your body is positioned. By looking down at my feet I can tell that they are in front of me and safe but if I were to travel without ankle straps and my foot were to slide off the plate, then I could be in danger of breaking my ankle or foot. This actually did happen to me as I was coming down a ramp and the front of my shoe was stubbed resulting in my foot twisting sideways and fracturing my ankle bone. I also use a

Velcro seat belt that keeps me positioned in my chair and stops me from being thrown if I stop quickly. Customized seating is necessary for anyone who is in a seated position for extended periods of time because of the danger of pressure sores. I am always fighting the risk of developing a decubitus on my tail bone or heels. This is a common occurrence for anyone with a spinal cord injury who has lost sensation in these areas. My paralysis has resulted many times in me developing a pressure sore. This would often mean not being able to sit up in my wheelchair or bed in order to relieve pressure on my tailbone. Obviously it is difficult to be productive in any way when you are required to lie in bed on your side or stomach.

My physician continued to increase the dosage of my anti-spasm medication as the spasms got worse. It was somewhat helpful in reducing the spasms but proved to be detrimental to my ability to go to classes and live a regular life. You see, this medication was a sedative to control my muscles but it also made me very drowsy. I can recall going to class and trying very hard to stay awake, only to wake up as the class was ending and not remember anything. I would find that I had drooled down my face and left a pool of spit on my desk or textbook. Initially I did not understand why I could not concentrate in class and wondered at times if I would ever be able to finish my degree.

Muscle spasms are very common in people with

spinal cord injuries. Medication can be somewhat helpful but counterproductive when the dosage is incorrect. After explaining my difficulties to my physician we decided to proceed with a surgical procedure called a rhizotomy. This is a procedure performed by a neurosurgeon and involves cauterizing the nerve ends in your back that are alongside the spinal cord. A needle is inserted into these nerve endings and burns them to kill any transmission of signals from the brain to accompanying body parts. I do not have sensation in my back so this procedure sounds much more painful than it was.

It was explained up front that this procedure could accomplish the desired outcome but was not always a permanent solution. It seemed rather ironic that I was now a quadriplegic because my spinal cord would not regenerate nerve cells, but the nerve roots I was willingly trying to make inactive had the ability to eventually regenerate and bring back muscle spasms. After completing this surgical procedure though, I would hopefully have less muscle spasming and would be able to reduce the amount of spasticity medicine that I was taking.

I was taken into the operating room of a local hospital and turned over lying down onto my stomach. I could not see what was happening as I was face down but I could hear voices around me. This neurosurgeon demanded his staff be on time and ready to proceed when he was. I became scared when he began to yell, and I didn't understand why he was angry. It seems that one of his staff was late and this was not acceptable to him.

Up to this point in dealing with my spinal cord injury, I had maintained a very small hope that some type of a cure would be developed and that I would be able to regain the physical capabilities that I had lost several years ago. Deciding to proceed with this surgical procedure, meant that I had accepted that I would not walk again. I was voluntarily letting someone kill the nerve roots, meaning they would never allow brain signals to readily transfer through my spinal cord into the rest of my body. I laid there wishing for a positive outcome to this procedure while I smelled the singeing of my burnt flesh where the needle had entered my back. Tears dripped from my eyes. I knew that this procedure would be beneficial to me as a quadriplegic, but it was something that I would never have allowed if I honestly felt there was continued hope for recovery.

Withdrawing from my medication for muscle spasms eventually helped to make me more alert and able to concentrate in classes. However, as I began to withdraw, I started to have seizures. The seizures would come at any time without warning. I recall during an afternoon trip to Pitt for class, I was wheeling through the student quadrangle alone and started to feel as if I was going to have a seizure. My body started to feel strange and a convulsion seemed to come from the inside. I stopped and sat in the middle of this large walkway afraid to move because I knew what was coming. I was by myself and felt like a fish out of water. Many students were passing by me, but I was too proud to ask for help because I really didn't know what any of them could do. Also, these seizures were very embarrassing to me and just returning back to school had been difficult enough. Dealing with the embarrassment of a seizure seemed even more unbelievable. As I looked around, I noticed a friend of mine who had been a member of the wrestling team with me. Billy Clark stopped and asked me if I was okay. Even though I wasn't sure what to do, at least I was comforted that I had a friend there that was willing to help. Fortunately, Billy was able to recline the back of my chair which may have prevented a seizure and I was able to eventually return home. This moment stands out in my mind because it made me realize that no matter how alone I felt, people in general will be glad to help if they realize you are in need.

Pursuing an Education

Going back to school several evenings a week, I was determined to earn a bachelor's degree, although I had no real idea of where this would take me or what I would do with it. At that time I did not know what my capabilities were both physically and mentally, so my future seemed very vague. However, pursuing an education gave me a goal. In my wrestling days, I would set goals for myself and work as hard as possible to accomplish them. Once each goal was met, I would set another goal with higher expectations and then work hard again to accomplish that goal. I applied this same determination to my life as a quadriplegic who was struggling to move forward.

Psychology intrigued me because the course work delved into many areas of self-analysis and I was able to relate my upbringing and family relationships to the studies. I decided to concentrate in psychology and pursue this with a bachelor's degree. However, I knew that this degree would not provide me with a career that would pay well enough for me to live comfortably, especially with my physical limitations. I knew that I would need to pursue a graduate degree in an area of concentration that would be both mentally and financially rewarding. That decision would come at a later time, but at this point I needed to accomplish my first goal.

It hadn't been easy going back to school with the many physical limitations that I had, along with the emotional feelings that I would face when running into old friends who had known me prior to my accident. I had lost connection with many of my former classmates and teammates. Some of them came around for a short while but then moved on with their own lives, as we all do. I was very fortunate to have one wrestling teammate from college that never forgot about me. He helped me when I returned to college and became my best friend. José Martinez was a wrestler whom I had first met when we both were recruited to the wrestling team as freshmen. He was a scrappy kid from Bethlehem, Pennsylvania that was in the same 126-pound weight class as me and was vying for a starting role on the varsity team. He was very outgoing and talked a lot about his high school wrestling team but not much about his family life. He was raised by his mother with many siblings but never discussed his father who lived in Puerto Rico and was not part of his upbringing. My personality was much more reserved and I envied his gregarious disposition. His Puerto Rican heritage was unique in the Pittsburgh-area as there were not many local Hispanic families. In my hometown of New Kensington, I do not recall knowing anyone who was

Puerto Rican, so he was a bit intriguing. He always had a story to tell about his friends or family back in Bethlehem that would make you laugh or sometimes wonder, "Can this be true?"

We had both been very dedicated to wrestling and unfortunately both wanted to win the starting varsity position for the 126-pound weight class. There were at least six wrestlers vying for this position and as we got closer to the start of our regular season, coach Dave Adams started to schedule wrestle-offs. These matches paired José and me against each other in the wrestling room. We were evenly-matched despite our physical differences and were both determined to win. José was short and quick like a cat, and I was taller with good leverage. One match became intense and heated as we both badly wanted to win. With the score tied midway through, we were near the edge of the mat and he pushed me into the padded wall as the whistle blew. Our tempers began to flare. I was fortunate to score the last point and win this initial challenge. At that point, we both didn't like each other very much! However, through this intense competition and rivalry in our freshman year of college, I gained much respect for José as I think he did for me. I guess I should mention that he beat me in our second match. He never lets me forget!

Our friendship developed from there and we shared many great times together. In my return to college in a wheelchair, he often assisted me in the classroom and took notes for me, if needed. He would attend classes of mine because he wanted to help and he truly cared about me. I recall taking a Greek philosophy course which I registered for as an elective but had no idea what I was about to study. José seemed to enjoy the course much more than I did, even though I was the one taking it for credits. My concentration would often wander and I sometimes had to struggle to stay focused. Knowing his personality, I now understand why he reveled in reviewing our lessons with me as he often could be very philosophical.

He had gotten to know my family quite well, especially my father. I know that my dad truly appreciated that I had a friend like José and he grew to love him like a son. Typically every Sunday, José would come to my apartment and together we would drive to my father's apartment in Monroeville, a town on the other side of Pittsburgh. All three of us would watch football on television and then my dad would take us out to dinner in a local restaurant. This became somewhat of a weekend tradition for us and it gave me something to look forward to away from school and medical appointments. I loved that my father was so welcoming to José and enjoyed spending this limited time with us. He became a father figure to José as his own father was not involved in his upbringing. I think that José truly enjoyed my friendship but also reveled in the affection that he felt from my father.

I was truly blessed to find a friend like José in college. There are people in your life who will have a great influence on your development. Our wrestling battles, our time together as teammates, the time he spent assisting me in classes and our time shared with my father have all shaped me in many positive ways. I have always remained good friends with José. He asked me to be the best man in his wedding which I was honored to do. We still often keep in touch and share memories of both good and bad times together.

I eventually earned enough credits to graduate with a bachelor's degree in August of 1982. This was much longer than the traditional four years required for a bachelor's degree but I guess it was a reasonable amount of time due to the many setbacks I had faced.

Jacob vs. YMCA

At the insistence of my father, shortly after my accident we had decided to file a personal injury lawsuit against the New Kensington YMCA. I was very hesitant to do this for several reasons. In the 1970s, personal injury lawsuits were not as common as they are today and were not viewed favorably by many. There was a stigma attached to filing a lawsuit against a nonprofit organization like the YMCA, especially one that I had grown up in and spent so many fond years as a kid. Also, filing a lawsuit against the YMCA meant naming specific individuals who were responsible for overseeing activities in the gymnasium the night of my accident. Moses Guin was the activities director and also the wrestling team coach. He was in the gym that night and was responsible for supervising all activities. He would be named as a responsible party in the lawsuit and I felt horrible about this and was a bit embarrassed to even make this claim. Like many of the other youth who had spent time growing up at the YMCA, I admired Moe. All of the kids liked Moe because we respected him but also knew that he cared about us. I never wanted to jeopardize my relationship with him or his employment at the YMCA. I never saw the accident as his fault, but the legal suit named him as being negligent for not properly supervising the situation.

My father hired an attorney from a respectable law firm in Pittsburgh. He told me that it was necessary for us to file this suit because we had to think about my future living with a disability and the financial resources I would need to assist me. My mother was opposed to filing the suit because of the stigma attached. I eventually conceded to my father and decided to take this action. It took several years for this claim to finally be settled because there was dispute about whether the claim had been initially filed in a timely manner and whether the two-year statute of limitations had expired. Also, there was much debate as to who was ultimately responsible.

We finally decided on a settlement that provided me with $190,000 after attorney fees were paid. In order to spread this payment out over a longer time we placed the money into a structured settlement that would provide me monthly payments for the next 20 years. In today's world of multi-million dollar awards, my settlement amount seems small for having to deal with such a severe and limiting disability for the remainder of my life. Sometimes I viewed it as a token payoff that never fairly compensated me for my medical needs, pain and suffering. Regardless of how much the settlement could have been, money would never return to me what I had lost. It did provide me with a small, regular source of income each month that proved to be very helpful as I was progressing through rehabilitation and during my many years of returning to school for my continued education. I hoped that the funds would assist me financially until I was able to obtain substantial employment and make an income that would support my lifestyle. I knew that this structured settlement would eventually run out and I could not rely upon it forever.

This settlement did provide me with the ability to make a down payment on a condominium that was located on South Highland Avenue near the University of Pittsburgh campus. It was close to school and a convenient commute to my classes. The mortgage payment was affordable for me with my monthly settlement and the salary I would eventually start making from my administrative residency. The income got my mother and me out of the government-subsidized apartment where we had been living in Blawnox for nearly six years after losing our apartment in Monroeville. Blawnox was a small suburb on the outskirts of Pittsburgh. It was not fancy, but it was safe.

I was very happy to finally move out of this apartment building in Blawnox because all of the people living there at that time were senior citizens. I felt out of place. I guess because many of the elderly residents had a lot of spare time on their hands, they liked to watch others in the building and were overly curious. Our apartment had two bedrooms but was not truly accessible because I was unable to get into the bathroom. We adapted by taking bed baths instead of using a regular shower so most of my daily hygiene care was done in the bedroom. When I wanted to wash my hair I had no choice but to go out of our apartment down the hall to the laundry room because there was a laundry sink that I could back my wheelchair up to. My mom would wrap my shoulders in a towel and we would head to the laundry room hoping that no one was using it at that time. I always felt a bit humiliated having to expose myself to people in the building for such a basic need that many take for granted.

I recall spending many summer days sitting on a rear patio of the building that was adjacent to a community park and softball field. I would overlook the field and watch the softball teams playing their games on weeknights and during the weekends. I often envied those young guys who enjoyed the friendly competition and camaraderie of their teammates. As a former athlete, I often sat there wishing that I could join in and step up to the plate trying to make that one hit or diving catch that would win the game. However, I would try not to dwell too long on fantasies because I realized that I needed to focus on what I had and not what I didn't.

Finding My Future Career

Finding a job with a bachelor's degree concentrating in psychology is difficult and if you do, chances are that it won't pay very well. As a quadriplegic, this task became much more difficult as I was unable to perform any job that required much physical ability. In addition, with the many medical expenses involved with my condition, I knew that I needed to find a job and career that would be financially-rewarding. I recognized that I would need to continue my education and pursue a graduate degree that would lead to a profession where I could use my mind and not my muscle.

I thought about becoming a licensed psychologist but truly was not empathetic enough to be in a job every day where I listened to other people's problems. I guess I felt that my problems were enough for me to handle, and I didn't want to handle someone else's, too. I considered pursuing an advanced degree in rehabilitation counseling. Rehabilitation counselors often work with individuals with disabilities and provide counseling to them relevant to vocational, social and professional issues. I knew that I had the capability to do this type of job, as I would be able to understand many of the issues, but I also knew that this field did not pay well and may not be able to support my needs. Also, I couldn't imagine spending the rest of my life counseling others who may have disabilities much less severe than mine, as I would have problems sympathizing with them. I began to look into pursuing law school and becoming a lawyer specializing in healthcare law. I was always intrigued by the legal profession and knew a professor who was a paraplegic and was very successful in his legal career as a trial attorney and law school professor. I admired his confidence to be in this role despite an obvious disability. I bought an LSAT preparatory textbook and began to study.

As happened quite often during that time, my quadriplegia brought about many physical conditions that made it difficult for me to accomplish my goals. The cold winters of Pittsburgh would often lead to me getting a cold which would affect my chest and lung capacity. My intercostal muscles (the muscles between the ribs that assist with breathing) are paralyzed and I am unable to cough well. Bronchitis and pneumonia are very dangerous to me as I don't have the ability to recuperate as easily as someone physically healthy. I would end up sick and eventually admitted into a hospital for these conditions. I must have been admitted at least six times to several of the local hospitals while pursuing my bachelor's degree. The more that I spent time in hospitals, the more intrigued I became with how these institutions functioned and how they treated patients like me. I received some very substandard care during several visits and began to question why the care could not be better. I figured that I had spent much time in hospital settings and maybe I would be able to take my experiences and observations and apply them towards improving hospital care.

I began to consider what it would take to become a hospital administrator. I figured that the pay would probably be substantial and that there hopefully would be many opportunities in a city the size of Pittsburgh to get a job. I was limited in where I would be able to go to pursue a graduate degree in healthcare administration, because I was living with my mother as my primary caretaker and could not easily relocate. Fortunately, the University of Pittsburgh offers a master's degree in healthcare administration from their Graduate School of Public Health. Researching this degree piqued my interest as I became sure that this was a career that I would enjoy, that could be financially rewarding and that I could be very good at. I submitted my application to the GSPH hoping to be accepted and start classes in the fall of 1983.

Much to my disappointment, I was not initially accepted into the MHA program because during those difficult years while earning my bachelor's degree, my grades were not high enough. The medication issues along with health problems contributed to several grades that did not impress the admissions department. I was devastated to learn that I was not accepted and could not imagine doing anything else at that time. Deciding not to give up, I was determined to reapply and find a way to pursue my education and career. As He had done before, I feel that God put someone in my path that would be able to assist me.

Gerry St. Denis, Assistant Director of Admissions of the Graduate School of Public Health, was a stately gentleman who had much influence in accepting applicants. He had been a professor for many years in this school, and I learned that he had a son who was a paraplegic due to a severe accident. His son had gone on to pursue law school and became successful in his life. I had the opportunity to meet with Dr. St. Denis and convey my sincere desire to earn an MHA and pursue a career in hospital administration. I think that he saw me as a young man, like his son, trying to make the most of his life who had the willpower to deal with the many obstacles and barriers ahead. He looked past my disability and was able to get the admissions committee to admit me on a trial basis, meaning that I would be permitted to take several courses in the school and if my grades were good then I would be reconsidered for admission. This was fantastic news. Dr. St. Denis gave me a second chance that I will always be grateful for. I was very fortunate at this crossroads in my life to have someone like him that understood the difficulties of spinal cord injury who was able to assist me in making the most of my life.

I started to take my first graduate classes a bit later than I had wanted because of this delay, but I quickly proved to Dr. St. Denis and the admissions committee that I had the capabilities to successfully earn my degree. After completing the initial classes with excellent grades, my application was accepted and I was a full-time graduate student. I knew that, given a chance, I would be able to keep up with the rigors of this program while dealing with my disability.

The Graduate School of Public Health was a large building eight-stories high that housed several departments including genetic counseling, epidemiology, biostatistics and health administration. Unfortunately, it was not wheelchair accessible and I had to enter the school through a side door that did not have steps. The front door and main entrance had several steps and prior to the Americans with Disabilities Act (ADA) there were no plans to change these entrances. I also learned that there had never been a wheelchair student like myself that had attended this school and graduated. Fortunately, again Dr. St. Denis made sure that I was provided with a key to this rear door and that I was permitted to park my van in a space near the garbage dumpster that was off-limits to others for parking. These small considerations made it possible for me to get into the school every day. My mother would drive me into Oakland every day and assist me getting into the building. She would often stay if I had only a few classes, or she would find things to do in the area and come back when I was finished.

I did not have enough strength or ability in my arms to write legibly, therefore when taking classes, I would often ask a classmate if I could copy their notes after class and use these to reference in the future. This was helpful for some classes that involved numbers and statistics because the professor would often stray from the lessons defined in the textbook. I eventually realized that it was simpler for me to maintain full concentration on the lecture without having to take notes and distract me from the lecture. I would go home in the evenings after each class and review the material as most of it was already defined in the textbook. This method of learning is what I used throughout graduate school and many people were surprised when I told them that I really didn't need to take notes. I was fortunate again to find classmates who would often go out of their way to assist me in any way possible — getting through large doorways that did not open automatically, working on joint projects, helping me with a drink of water or many other tasks that seemed so small to others but very difficult for me.

The Master's of Health Administration program was very demanding as I was required to complete 60 credits of coursework, a three-month internship, a one-year residency within a health care institution, and a Master's thesis to earn my degree. The fieldwork and thesis added another 12 credits which meant a full 72 credits over three years going full-time. Most graduate degrees are not this demanding, and I sometimes questioned why I chose the one that seemed to require more time and effort than all others that I had considered.

Going to graduate school not only provided me with an excellent education to help me prepare for a career in the healthcare industry, but it also instilled in me an increased sense of confidence in myself and my abilities. This is something that I had lost after my accident because I had felt very unattractive. Like most 24-year-old males, I still felt that the most important attribute to attracting women was a good physique and handsome face. In my disabled condition, I no longer felt that I was attractive to women as my muscular physique had atrophied and I no longer looked handsome. My mother encouraged me to meet girls at school and possibly develop a relationship. I would often cry and tell her that I couldn't imagine a woman who would want me in my condition. I had no money, could not drive and lived in a senior citizen high-rise apartment with my mother. She would disagree and tell me that someday I would find a woman to love me because she knew something that I didn't realize at that time.

The more time that I spent in graduate school, the more that I began to suspect my mother was right and that women my age could be attracted to me. While doing my graduate internship at St. Margaret's Hospital, I became attracted to a cute, young nurse. Every time I saw her at the hospital, my crush became even stronger. I would often see her in the cafeteria but was too shy to have much conversation with her. I overheard her talking with a friend and discussing their plans for the weekend. They talked about things they would be doing that I would've loved to be involved with. That day when I returned to my apartment, I sat out on the patio with my sister Amy and talked about this nurse. Amy always had a sympathetic ear for me, and I was happy to be able to talk to someone. The more I talked, the more I cried. I felt so helpless to change my situation and didn't think that I would ever enjoy the companionship of a woman again. She cried along with me and assured me that our mother was right and someday this would change.

It was later in graduate school that I met a girl who flagrantly flirted with me and seemed interested in what I was doing. Maybe earlier there had been girls interested in me but I never recognized the flirting because of my lack of self-confidence. She was a very nice girl who had just been accepted into the Pitt medical school and would be starting soon. I was not certain why she would be interested in me because she was obviously very intelligent and I was certain she could find another boyfriend. Nothing ever came of my interactions with this girl, but it did help me to realize that as a young man earning a very respectable degree, I just might be attractive to women for numerous reasons beyond a desirable physique.

After completing two full years of coursework, I was required to do a one-year health administration residency in a healthcare institution of my choice. I had always been very interested in returning back to the Harmarville Rehabilitation Center for this residency as this was the institution where I had spent over six months as a patient several years before. After a successful interview, I was accepted to start my residency in the fall of 1985.

Once again, I feel that God put someone into the path of my life. Lee Lacey was the President/CEO of Harmarville and would serve as my preceptor during this year of residency. He was an amazing person and a strong advocate for people with disabilities. He saw my abilities and gave me a chance to learn from him. Many of my peers from graduate school were not involved in residency programs that gave them an opportunity to spend much time with the CEO of an institution. Mine was much different because Mr. Lacey made a concerted effort to involve me in all aspects of administering this business and running a multimillion dollar company. Initially it was a bit scary to return to Harmarville as an administrative student. Eventually my feelings evolved, and I began to feel great about the opportunity to be seen in a much different light from when I was a patient there. The setting was perfect for me because staff were very familiar with dealing with people with disabilities, I had an opportunity to learn from an excellent role model, and I truly enjoyed working around many nurses and therapists near my age.

I recall the first day of starting my residency very vividly. My mother dressed me in my best gray suit and drove me to the front entrance. On the radio played a song that is very near and dear to my mother, "Like a Rock" by Bob Seeger. She always related me to this song as she felt my determination was like a rock. As I rolled off of the wheelchair ramp and entered through the automatic electric doors, I could see her behind me with teary eyes, a big smile and a great sense of pride. She had gotten me to this point in my life and I was prepared to start the next chapter.

Harmarville Rehabilitation Center

I was returning back to the facility that had cared for me for nearly seven months after my injury and helped me to start my life over again as a quadriplegic. This was the place that I was admitted to lying flat on my back and scared as hell about what my future would hold. I now had an opportunity to return as a graduate student and look at this facility from a completely different perspective.

This environment was ideal for me because of the wheelchair accessibility features and the very caring and understanding staff. Some recognized me as a previous patient and others knew me as the son of Abraham Jacob, former director of the physical therapy department. I didn't know what my preceptor Lee Lacey had planned for me to do as a resident, but I was willing to work hard at any task that I was given in an attempt to prove that I could be as productive as anyone without a disability. Mr. Lacey provided me with an accessible desk placed outside of his office where I could be readily available when needed. I was included in all levels of administration and attended meetings throughout the facility involving every aspect of the organization. It was a great opportunity for me to learn the inner workings of a rehabilitation facility and what was involved with operating this type of business. Most importantly, I was able to closely observe the managerial style of Mr. Lacey and absorb the values that he instilled in his administrative staff. It was obvious to me and everyone around him that he loved his job. He would pass by my desk at times whistling happily on his way to another meeting and always took the time to talk with employees as he made his way along. Like many of the other employees at Harmarville, I greatly respected him and admired his sense of dedication to the organization. He treated his employees like they were a part of his family and we all felt like he truly cared about us.

I recall a board of directors meeting that I was attending where Mr. Lacey wanted to send approximately 10 employees with physical disabilities to an international conference in Europe. He had requested funds for this trip from the Board of Directors which amounted to over $15,000. In 1985 this was a sizable chunk of money and several of the board members including the chairman were resistant to approving this spending. They could not recognize the value of sending these disabled employees to an international conference that would have no immediate return on investment. Mr. Lacey saw things differently. He knew that many of these employees had never had a chance — and probably never would — to travel overseas on their own and attend this type of conference. He knew that their dedication to Harmarville was very valuable and he wanted this to be recognized. This type of dedication was not uncommon for the many employees who worked under his supervision. He conveyed this type of family culture to the organization and it was returned many times over. After a long debate with the board chairman, Mr. Lacey stated that if the organization was not willing to approve this funding then he would be willing to do it out of his own personal finances. This personal commitment made the board members realize how strongly he cared about the value of these employees and proceeded to approve full funding. I learned a very valuable lesson that day from Mr. Lacey. Having care for his employees and the fulfillment of the organization's mission resulted in a very successful business. I hoped that someday I would be able to convey these principles wherever I worked.

Every day I would wear a suit and tie to my residency as I wanted to be seen as an administrative resident and not in my previous capacity as a patient. I was able to work with one of the occupational therapists at the facility who provided me with a writing splint that was placed into my right hand so that I could begin writing again. I had regained enough use of my right shoulder muscle that I was able to crudely move my arm and splint with it. However, my right hand and fingers did not move. This was new for me as I didn't do much writing while I was in graduate school and had actually gotten used to keeping notations in my mind rather than on paper. However, my residency required me to maintain a schedule that had various meetings at different times throughout the large facility. Having a pen to jot down schedules was helpful and I began to use the splint often. I recall that the first pen placed into my splint had red ink. When I made notations on any memos or documents given to me, it looked like I was a schoolteacher making corrections on test papers. Mr. Lacey kidded with me several times when I returned documents back to him annotated with red ink.

The downside of this writing splint was that I needed assistance with placing the writing splint into my regular wrist splint, and once it was put into place it was simpler to just leave it there rather than taking it off and on. This resulted in me entering various departments and meetings representing hospital administration wearing a suit and carrying a pen at all times with a notebook on my lap. For those who did not know me, it was suspected that I was surveying their work and would be reporting this back to the CEO. I often wondered why people treated me with a sense of suspicion and carefully chose their words around me when I entered a meeting. It amused me that here I was, the same guy who several years ago could barely sit up straight in therapy for more than an hour at a time, now being seen as an authority figure. I wanted to be treated like any other employee but did enjoy the respect that I was given.

Harmarville employed many young physical, occupational, and speech therapists, as well as counselors and nurses. Much to my liking, many of these professions were predominantly female and this gave me an opportunity to interact and work with many young, single women. As a 27-year-old single guy who had not dated for seven years, I was ready to maybe find someone that would be interested in me. I had started to gain more confidence in myself and began to accept that a woman may actually be interested in me.

A young occupational therapist student caught my eye one day standing in the long corridor near the occupational therapy department. Paige Huneycutt was a 21-year-old doing a four-month clinical affiliation as part of her academic curriculum with the Medical College of Georgia. She was in her senior year of her bachelor's degree and had chosen Harmarville for this student affiliation because of its excellent reputation. After several random passings, I gathered enough courage to stop and talk with her. Her southern accent and friendly smile made me very interested in getting to know her better. I had been out of the dating scene for many years and was uncertain if our conversations meant that she was also interested in me. We began to talk frequently and I sensed that she liked being around me. I noticed that she wore a ring on her left hand but never spoke about a fiancé or any love in her life. I was rather naïve about engagements so simply assumed that whoever had given her the ring was in the past. We would sometimes go to lunch together in the cafeteria and I invited her to visit me at the small high-rise apartment that I shared with my mother.

Living arrangements were typically organized through Harmarville and the student's school. She was living in a nearby community in the house of an elderly woman.. It was October and the cooler weather was starting. Paige's family lived in Miami. I remember thinking that she must hate being in Southwestern Pennsylvania and having to deal with cold weather. I had never been to Georgia where she went to school before so thought that it was warm there all year long. As an out-of-state student, she did not know anyone from the area and was happy to have a friend with whom to explore and visit local sites. We started to date and I had a great time sharing my familiarity of Pittsburgh with an out-of-towner. The more time that we spent together, the closer we got and our friendship eventually turned into a romance.

She was not shy about dealing with my disability and physical limitations. I had not had a girlfriend in a long time and the relationship that I had with Paige made me realize that I was still an attractive young man who could be desirable to women. This newfound sense of confidence would shape my future and my ability to interact once again with women despite my disability.

She was to complete her student affiliation by the middle of December and return back to the Medical College of Georgia in Augusta. I knew that this time would eventually come but chose not to dwell on it and instead truly enjoyed the time that we had spent together.

It was nearing the middle of December and the annual Christmas party for all employees of Harmarville was being held at the Carnegie Museum in Oakland, a suburb of Pittsburgh. It was a beautiful setting for a wonderful party that included a live band and much dancing on the large marble floors. Paige and I went as a couple and as we made our way across the dance floor, I bumped into another young woman who I recognized from work. I couldn't remember her name but knew her beautiful smile. She seemed so happy to see me there. We exchanged greetings amid the loud music and moved on. Paige was behind me and must have noticed this woman's interest in me but nothing was ever said. I was pleasantly surprised that another attractive woman besides Paige had shown interest in me. I guess I knew that ultimately my relationship with Paige would not last forever. When she returned to school, I was heartbroken. We kept in touch over the phone, but we both needed to complete our educational degrees and knew that it was near impossible to maintain a long-distance relationship.

The Love of My Life

Linda Glovier, one of the older secretaries in the administrative area where my desk was located, was participating in a sign language class. She and other employees would get together at the end of the day and practice what they were learning. This is where Linda formally introduced me to Jamie Gaydos, the young woman that I had run into on the dance floor at the company Christmas party. I remember being intrigued by her because her beautiful smile would light up the room, and she always seemed so positive. I was always attracted to girls who were intelligent and displayed a sense of confidence. This was Jamie exactly!

She graduated at the top of her Freeport High School class and summa cum laude from the Indiana University of Pennsylvania. While in high school, she was the winner of the local Junior Miss Pageant and was the Pennsylvania State runner-up. When I first met her, I didn't realize how perfect she was for me and how much she was everything that I had always hoped to find. She was a newly-hired rehabilitation counselor working in the vocational rehab department. Her job entailed working with many spinal cord injured patients like myself and helping them to pursue education and obtain future employment. Her constant energy and positive outlook made her a great counselor for these patients who were so in need of her abilities.

Much to my surprise, one day when returning to my desk, I found a handwritten note stating "I stopped by to see if you wanted to get some coffee with me". It was signed by Jamie. I didn't know what to think. First of all, I was still getting over Paige returning back to Georgia. Secondly, I didn't know if she was just being cordial and offering me help or if she had some interest in me. I was intrigued that she actually wanted to talk with me socially, not related to work. Since I had spent several months feeling lonely, my mother suggested that I follow up with the girl that left me the note. She asked me, "What do you have to lose?" and convinced me that it was worth the effort. Actually, I think she knew that Jamie was the answer to my wishes and her prayers.

I began to go to lunch with Jamie and her supervisor Debbie on a fairly regular basis in the cafeteria. I got to know her better through these casual lunches and became more interested in her. I also began to sense that she enjoyed being around me. I decided to ask her to meet me at a local restaurant for brunch on a Sunday in March and she agreed. My mother dropped me off at the restaurant. Jamie was already waiting inside. It was very strange to be a mid-20s man having your mother drop you off for a date with a woman. I didn't have many other options, but Jamie didn't seem to mind and never made me feel uncomfortable. As I pulled up to the table, the foot rest of my wheelchair projected forward and the only way for me to get comfortably under the table would be to manually swing away the foot rest. I assumed that she would know how to do this, but she had never had to make this type of adjustment with any of her patients. As she struggled to find the right lever to press, I felt embarrassed that she had to be nearly under the table fumbling with my wheelchair on our first date. She didn't seem phased and smiled while laughing it off making me feel comfortable. This was a true indication of the outgoing personality and charm that made me quickly fall in love with her.

We began to spend every weekend together as we had much in common and similar interests. She liked sports, and I was a former jock. This gave us a large array of sporting activities to follow, living in the Pittsburgh area. Pittsburgh is a sports town and there is a continuous array of professional and collegiate sports to follow throughout the year. Jamie also liked theater and drama and had been involved with high school musicals as part of her younger activities. My mother had piqued my interest in theater when I was in elementary school with the local civic theater group. She enrolled my brother and I in several plays. We had only small parts, but I enjoyed being part of the cast and performing on stage. Our similar experiences and interest in live theater gave us another activity that we enjoy doing together. I had season tickets for the Pittsburgh Public Theater, a reputable professional group in our area. We enjoyed going to theater performances and always looked forward to this formal date. I found over time that being with Jamie made me a stronger person and able to better deal with my disability.

After a few years of attending these performances, we had an experience that was difficult to deal with and reinforced to me that many people do not understand the difficulties and personal pressures of being in public with an electric wheelchair. Jamie and I entered the PPT theater and took our regular seats on the floor level in anticipation of the play starting soon. As we sat there, the theater filled up and we anxiously waited for the first act. This was a theater-in-the-round which meant that the seats rose on three sides of the stage so that everyone would have a good view. Sitting on the floor level in the first row, we were clearly visible to everyone in the theater. Typically these performances started right on time but for some reason this night we were delayed about 10 minutes. Everyone was in their seats and anxious for the play to start, but it was being held up by the performance director. I recall an employee of the theater approaching me and telling me that I would not be able to sit in this location because I would be in the way of the actors entering and exiting the stage. I was told that they could not start the play until I had moved. He asked if I could go out into the lobby and watch the performance from the television set located there. They had not set the stage up to accommodate a wheelchair, and I would inhibit the performance. I was not opposed to moving my location but was appalled that they requested me to sit in the lobby and watch a live performance on a television monitor. Jamie was very angry with the request and was adamant about not moving due to their improper planning. I was very embarrassed because the full theater of people were watching us as this situation unfolded. After a standoff of about five minutes with having the eyes of all in the theater glaring upon us, we decided to leave our location so that the show could go on for the other patrons.

As I rolled out into the lobby, I was overcome with feelings of sadness and anger. I was embarrassed that I had been segregated from the physically-able audience members and singled out of a large crowd due to my wheelchair. After a serious accident and change in your physical appearance, it is very difficult to adjust and accept people looking at you. I had never been treated differently from people around me in such an obvious manner. Part of me felt ashamed and angry because I knew that my life in a wheelchair was going to be much more difficult than I wanted to accept. Jamie knew that I had been hurt and could see it in my eyes as they swelled with tears. We decided to quickly leave the theater and pledged to never go back again.

After much thought and time to digest the situation, I decided to write a letter to the appropriate people involved with the Pittsburgh Public Theater organization. I explained how I had been a longstanding member of the PPT and felt that I had been discriminated against. I knew that this was a very reputable organization and included many of the most prominent people in the Pittsburgh area, including several who were physically disabled. I wanted them to know how I had felt because of the actions taken by their staff. I felt that I needed to advocate for myself and for other people with disabilities so that this type of situation would not happen again in the future. I wanted to know that when I showed up for a performance that there would be an accessible seating area for me and that no one would have the right to make me move from it.

After a few days, I received a phone call from a representative of the PPT who was extremely apologetic and promised that if I wished to return in the future I would receive season tickets at no cost for many years. I was very happy that their organization recognized how this situation had affected me, Jamie and many others in the theater that night. I found out that they had received other letters and complaints from people who were there and had seen what happened to me. It made me feel good to know that the people I was concerned about looking at me that night were the same people who came to my defense and demanded action be taken so that this would never happen again. Is life fair? Here is a bad situation that turned out well for me. Sometimes when things don't seem fair, I keep my feelings in perspective and recognize that life is not what's given to you but what you make of it.

Jamie's and my relationship began to develop very quickly. Within the first months of dating, we became very affectionate and began to get physically involved. She had recently graduated from college and was working in her first job at the Harmarville Rehabilitation Center. Several months before I had met her, she had found an apartment in a close neighboring town with her friend Jennifer. Unfortunately for me, the apartment was on the third floor of a complex that had no elevator. This meant that if we wanted to stay together it had to be in my place and not hers. She began to stay overnight with me at my apartment in a subsidized highrise in Blawnox. As a poor college student I didn't have much money and it was definitely not fancy but fulfilled my needs at the time. It was a small two-bedroom apartment that my mother and I shared as she was my primary caretaker. My mother was always very open-minded about having Jamie stay over with me although it was a bit awkward knowing that she was aware of my romantic interests. I knew that my mother was happy to see me making every effort to live the normal life of a young man in his mid-20s and that my relationship with Jamie was welcomed by her.

Jamie was much different than any girlfriend I had ever had before. She enjoyed doing things for me and giving things to me. I have always referred to her as "a giver" because this is what makes her happy. All of my previous girlfriends had enjoyed getting things from me and probably expected it from me. I liked to give small gifts to my girlfriends and had always accepted that this was only normal. After dating for only a few months, on Easter Sunday, Jamie surprised me with a beautiful Easter basket filled with small items and candies that she knew I enjoyed. I had never been given such a personalized gift from a girlfriend that expressed her care and warmth. I was very surprised by her efforts and this made me realize how much she cared about me despite my physical limitations. I began to believe that Jamie and I were in love and that our relationship was something that I had never had before.

Shortly after we started dating, Jamie wanted me to see her parent's house where she had grown up in the rural Sarver Area. I guess that she wanted me to know more about her and her background. These were the roots of her upbringing and she wanted me to understand where she came from and begin to know her family. Since my time in a wheelchair, I had never gone to a girlfriend's house and I had to deal with accessibility issues. Her family had a one-story ranch house that had several steps to get into the front door but only one to get into the back door.

One evening we got into my accessible van and headed out to Sarver. We parked in the gravel driveway and headed up a large, grassy embankment to get around the house to the back. When we arrived in the back there was a piece of plywood that had been placed at the step to serve as a ramp for my wheelchair. In advance of us coming, Jamie had asked her dad Joe to find a board that would allow me to have access into their house. Her father was always the person that would do anything to help and please his daughters. He probably never gave a second thought to ramping his rear door for this unknown friend of Jamie's that was in a wheelchair. Little did he know that this was going to be the start of something very different, but special, in his daughter's life. Surprisingly, no one was at home when we arrived and it seemed a bit strange sitting in this small ranch house out in a rural area alone with Jamie.

Much of her family lived within the surrounding area. Her grandparents John and Anna owned a small house and farm less than a half mile from her parents. This is where her father was raised along with his four siblings. Despite the house being small, there was always room for everyone at Sunday Slovak dinners cooked by Anna. I was quickly welcomed into this household and always felt comfortable around her family. I initially feared that it would be awkward for me, but her grandmother greeted me with open arms. Joe was the oldest, followed by his three sisters and youngest brother. He was the big brother who everyone relied upon, and he always made himself available to help. They all lived a very modest lifestyle and never moved far from this area.

Her dad worked as a technician at the Alcoa Aluminum Research Center in New Kensington where he had met Jamie's mother Jean Nicastro. She had worked there as a secretary and was originally from Arnold, PA until she moved to Sarver after they were married. They had two children starting with Barbara who was about three years older than Jamie. All four of them lived there happily, but unfortunately during Jamie's teenage years her mother developed mental health problems.These issues forced Joe to care for her while assuming many of the responsibilities of raising two daughters.

Jamie and I began to spend time together just about every day because during the weekdays we worked at the same place, saw each other during lunch and always planned our weekend activities together. She was never afraid to do anything. I was always fearful that no woman would ever want me as a disabled person because of my dependence upon her. It never seemed that way with Jamie. She welcomed the opportunity to help me whenever I had a need

— and as a quadriplegic I had many of them. I was unable to transfer in and out of bed, dress myself, groom myself and feed myself independently. Jamie had never been trained as a nurse but had no reservations about learning how to assist me with these functions and take on these responsibilities. As we started to spend time alone without the assistance of my mother, it was necessary for her to assist me with these functions if we were to go anywhere alone for a longer period of time. After some very awkward training on changing my urinal catheter from my mother, Jamie and I felt that we were ready to try our first weekend alone. You can imagine how awkward it felt for me as a 27-year-old man having his mother teaching his girlfriend how to change the external catheter on my penis. UGHH!

We made weekend reservations for a hotel in Erie, Pennsylvania thinking that this would be a nice opportunity for us to spend time alone and really test how compatible we might be. I was afraid that after spending a weekend alone with me she would do an about-face and run for the hills as fast as she could. I think she also wanted to test her own abilities to see if she could handle the responsibilities of caring for a quadriplegic. Shortly after we arrived in Erie, we went to dinner and then back to the hotel. Our room was located on the first floor and had a large sliding glass door out onto a patio that led to a grassy area and pool. While sitting in the room, I suddenly heard a knock coming from the glass door but was unable to see who it was because the curtains were closed. Jamie cautiously opened the curtains and standing there was her father Joe. He had made the two-hour trip to Erie to check up on his daughter and make sure all was okay. It was a good thing that she and I had not been involved in doing anything that could have been embarrassing to us and her father. I look back now and laugh about this time because I realized that he was concerned about his daughter but also because he wanted to be the prankster and shock the hell out of me. I have now grown to be very close with Joe because he is a great father to Jamie and I am very thankful that he welcomed me into his family and their lives.

The more time that Jamie and I spent together, the more comfortable we both felt. When she went back to her apartment after weekends on Sunday evenings, I missed her until I saw her the next day at work. Within four months of dating we had fallen in love and I knew that this was the woman I wanted to spend the rest of my life with. I compulsively decided that I was going to ask her to marry me. On a Saturday morning I went to a jewelry store in New Kensington with Tony Carino, a personal aide who had become a friend of mine. I obviously did not have much experience in buying an engagement ring and chose one that was affordable to me and hopefully acceptable to Jamie. I made reservations for the next Saturday night at a fancy

French restaurant in Shadyside, a chic suburb of Pittsburgh. I told Jamie that we were going to go out and it would be a special night. I guess I should have never hinted because it gave away my surprise.

After finishing the main course, I directed her to go into my backpack and pull out a small box. I had no way of pulling the ring box out myself so had to ask for her to pull out and open her own engagement ring! I assume she suspected that this was an engagement ring because we had previously talked about the possibility of being together for a long time. Sitting at the restaurant table, she opened the box and I asked her to marry me. Her eyes filled with tears as she put the ring onto her own finger and she responded to me, yes! Looking into her smiling face, my eyes welled with tears of joy. I felt like I was the luckiest man in the world!

Prior to my accident and disability I had envisioned that someday when I asked a woman to marry me I would take the common approach of getting down on one knee and slipping the engagement ring onto her finger. I had never imagined that I would be sitting in a wheelchair giving directions and watching her place the ring on herself. I wished that it could have been that way, but that was not my life or story. The reality was that I had found a woman who loved me just the way I was. She was not caught up in all of the traditional expectations of a "normal" proposal but instead was excited that I had asked her to be my wife. We decided that we would get married in the next year; both of us wanted a summer wedding. This would give us plenty of time to prepare and make plans for where we would live.

We soon made a trip to her parent's home in Sarver and proceeded to tell them that we had exciting news. Standing in the middle of their living room, Jamie told them about my proposal and our marriage plans. Her dad was standing at the time and slowly backed up in order to sit down on the couch. I think that he was shocked to hear that she was willing to marry a quadriplegic, recognizing that this was a future that did not seem very inviting at that time. Her mother, Jean, was already sitting down but I could hear her say in a quite shocked tone, "Oh, Jamie". I now recognize that it was impulsive of me to ask Jamie to marry me without first giving her parents time to get to know me better. In fairness to them, if we had dated for a more prolonged time they could have gotten to know more about me and my character. I wish that I would have given them that opportunity to better understand me and recognize how much I loved their daughter. She and I had only known each other for four months, and I am sure they had never envisioned their daughter marrying someone with so many physical limitations. Fortunately for me, they did not oppose our marriage because they knew that Jamie was a very intelligent young woman and that she would never agree to a marriage unless she was truly in love.

Abraham and Jacqueline Jacob family photo.
(Left to right) Amy, Mom, Tony, Dad, Jeff,
Jill and Brian. 1966

Class of 1976 senior photo
Valley High School,
New Kensington, PA.
Brian at age 16.

University of Pittsburgh
wrestling team photo,
freshman year. 1977

Brian and his father Abraham on graduation day for his Master's degree in Healthcare Administration from the University of Pittsburgh. 1986

Jamie and Brian, newly engaged in the summer of 1986. He had broken his femur and was in a full leg cast.

Governor Richard Thornburgh, speaking,
presenting a check of $250,000 to Brian to
start a vocational rehabilitation agency.
Mr. Lee Lacey, president of Harmarville
Rehabilitation Center is on the far left. 1987

Wedding of Brian to Jamie Ann Gaydos
St. Joseph Church. Cabot, PA.
June 13, 1987

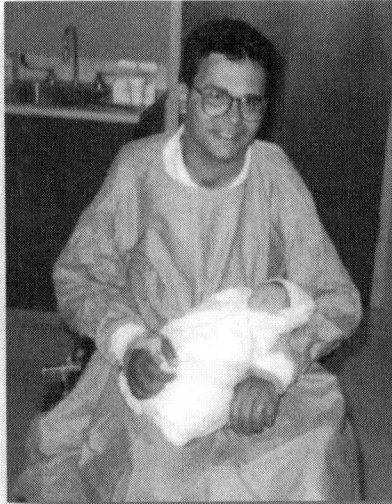

Birth of Brady Abraham Jacob in
Hickory, North Carolina.
August 3, 1989

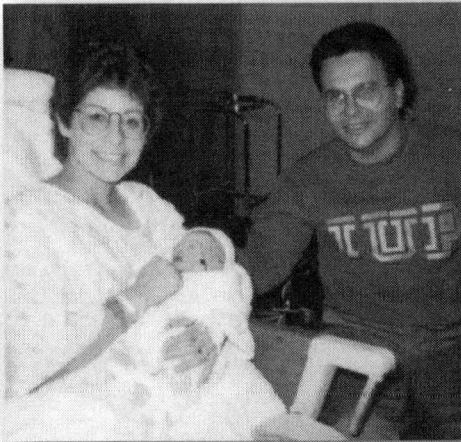

Birth of Maria Elise Jacob with Mom and Dad.
January 2, 1992

Brian as a proud papa with Maria, a few weeks old, and Brady, almost two-and-a-half years old. 1992

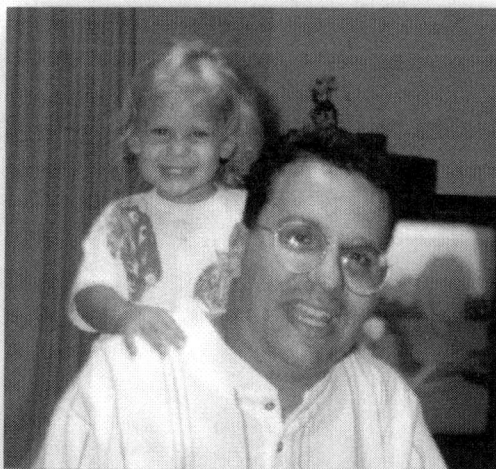

Maria riding on the back of Brian's wheelchair. 1995

Family photo in our home
Lower Burrell, Pennsylvania.
1997

Brian making his wedding toast to his daughter Maria
and her new husband Grant Mallory at the Pittsburgh
Botanical Gardens on September 2, 2017.

Jamie, Brady, Brian, Maria and Grant
on a Baltic Sea cruise. 2018

Graduation and Beyond

After several years of coursework, a summer internship, a year-long residency and completion of a Master's thesis, I was now ready to graduate. It had been a very long and demanding time for me in graduate school, but I knew that it had been a necessity for me to have a professional career with an attractive income. The graduation ceremony was scheduled in the spring of 1986 to be held at the Civic Arena in Downtown Pittsburgh. This facility has since been torn down and replaced by a more accessible entertainment facility. Pitt is a large university that had many of their undergraduate and graduate schools commencing on the same day. I recall most of the central floor area being filled with graduating students with the surrounding seats accommodating their families and friends.

I initially did not want to attend the ceremony because I didn't really recognize the importance of this day for me or my parents. For them it was a proud day to celebrate this accomplishment that they had both contributed to. I always maintained an attitude that I should be able to do the same or more than anyone else despite my disability, so I didn't really recognize this as being anything out of the ordinary. In reality, I did have to overcome many more obstacles and deal with many issues that were not ordinary because of my disability.

At the time, Jamie and I had been dating for a short while and I invited her to attend the graduation day ceremonies with my sister Amy, my mother and father. I was given a dark blue robe that had a traditional cape along with a graduate hat and tassel. I had never worn any of this before because I did not attend the graduation ceremony when I earned my undergraduate degree. No one had told me how this cap and gown was to be worn and the cape was only provided to Master's or doctorate degree students. Jamie had agreed to stay with me in the corridor while preparing to go onto the main floor to receive my degree. She started to help me put the robe over top of my head and we both realized that we had no idea if I was being dressed properly with the gown, cape and cap. In her nervousness to get this right, she began to seek advice from someone else in the corridor. She turned to a man coming out of a closed door and asked him if this was the right manner in which these clothes were to be worn. He politely replied that he did not know and walked in the other direction. I noticed that he was wearing a janitorial uniform. I told her that I didn't think he was the best person to ask as I expected he had never worn this type of garb. In her innocence, she was only asking for help from a stranger that she would have gratefully given to anyone else in need. That was the kind of person that she was.

As my name was called I sheepishly rolled down the aisle feeling that there were many eyes upon me. I heard a cheer coming from the upper seats that I knew was from my family. I was just one of thousands of graduates that day but when the chancellor set my diploma on my lap, I felt a special mix of pride and accomplishment that I never thought I would feel. My mother later told me that when my name was called and I came forward, my father's eyes began to water as he watched me. He was a man who did not cry very often and this indicated to me that it was something very special to him. The thought that I had made my parents and family proud was quite satisfying. I had accomplished something that they never thought I would be able to, and I had a brief moment to celebrate with them.

My father took all of us to dinner that afternoon and we all laughed together talking about the graduation robe and Jamie assisting me putting it on. Earning this graduate degree had been a very difficult and long journey for me but sitting together that night made it all feel worthwhile. I knew that my parents were proud of me because I had finally accomplished this goal that I had set for myself several years prior. Having achieved that, I now set my next goal a little higher and aimed to become employed and start a career where I could utilize my abilities and education.

Our Wedding and Honeymoon

We both wanted a summer wedding and set the date for the following year, June 13, 1987. We were married in the Catholic Church that she attended growing up. Saint Joseph's was a beautiful small church located in Cabot, Pennsylvania that was completely wheelchair accessible except for one step to get up to the altar. Once again, her father had an aluminum ramp made to get up this step so that I could be on the altar to make our vows in front of all of our family and friends.

That day started with rain. By the time I left with my brother Jeff to head to the church that afternoon, I was blessed with clear skies. It had become a beautiful June day. I had asked my younger brother Tony to be my best man because of our close relationship even though Jeff was closer in age to me. All through the morning and even when arriving at the church, I was not nervous. I was happy for this day to come. The wedding was scheduled for 3 PM. As Tony and I sat in the private room in the back of the church waiting for the time to come, I felt calm in my rented, white-jacketed tuxedo and red bowtie. All was fine until I heard the bell tower of the church begin to ring three times signaling it was now 3 PM. I recall thinking to myself that this was it, the day and time had finally come. I then became nervous as I wheeled down the aisle seeing the church full of friends, family and some strangers. I went up the ramp, turned around and took my position waiting for my future wife to arrive. The practiced keyboard music started to play and as I saw Jamie's smiling face as she came down the aisle on her father's arm, I began to cry. She was wearing her mother's wedding gown and a small veil that faintly covered her face. I was very embarrassed to cry but couldn't contain my happiness knowing that we were going to be married. When she arrived at the altar, she wiped my tears with her white-gloved hand and I no longer felt nervous. I smiled throughout the ceremony and felt like the luckiest guy in the world.

After the priest announced us as husband and wife, we turned around for the ceremonial march down the aisle. Jamie's wedding gown was long enough that it reached the floor in the back and made it hard for me to stroll close to her. Our first steps together as a married couple became awkward as her dress became entangled in my wheel. When she felt the tug along her side she stopped and I knew that something was wrong. I looked down to my side and saw her dress completely caught in my wheel and belt assembly. I tried to back up to untangle her dress carefully but instead my brother Jeff jumped in and tried helping. In this moment of panic, he pulled the dress and ripped the frail lace that was trapped in my wheel. We laughed at the situation and continued with our march up the aisle moving carefully so that her gown was not too close to my side. It was a moment that was indicative of our life to follow which would be full of unpredictable events that we would always deal with and overcome because of our very strong love for each other.

Our wedding reception was held in a pleasant but unpretentious facility in Lower Burrell that was paid for mostly by our fathers. To the nearly two hundred guests we offered a variety of foods that matched our heritages and the traditions of a southwestern Pennsylvania wedding reception. This always meant that a large "cookie table" was available to everyone in addition to the wedding cake. These cookies were made by many of the family members and offered a variety of everyone's favorites. My father's family was Syrian so in addition to the chicken and rigatoni we also had kibbee on the menu. We arranged for a live band to play our favorite music including our first dance song, "Just the Way You Are" by Billy Joel. It always seemed so appropriate to me because Jamie accepted me just the way I was despite my disability. It was very emotional for us to have our first dance together as husband and wife. Jamie sat on my lap as I whirled around the floor spinning left and right seeing the many faces around us smiling and crying as they watched us. This was one of the happiest days of my life. I smiled so much that my face hurt by the end of the day. Having all of my family and friends together to celebrate our marriage was a day I will never forget.

After our dance together and saying goodbye to all of our guests, we left the reception and traveled in my full size van with Jamie driving still in her wedding dress. As we headed down Route 28 towards the condominium we would have as our new home, someone started honking their horn behind us. Our friends from the wedding, Russ and Debbie Kuntz saw the "Just Married" and "Aloha" signs decorating the back door. We still laugh about this funny scene to this day.

We decided to travel to San Francisco and then to Maui, Hawaii for our honeymoon. Neither of us had ever been to these destinations and we were eager to see these sites together. At that time, I had a wheelchair that I used for traveling. It was able to be folded up and had a portable electric motor that could be strapped onto the back of the chair for mobility. This motor was placed into its own hard-shelled suitcase and transported separately from the wheelchair. It wasn't ideal but served the purpose for me to have electric motorized power whenever arriving at a foreign location. Portable wheelchair transportation has progressed much since that time.

We quickly learned that San Francisco was very hilly and difficult to get around with a portable electric wheelchair. Often Jamie had to push to get me up steep hills as we explored different areas around our hotel. None of this was easy and we were anxious to get to Maui as we hoped it would have a flatter terrain. When we arrived in Maui we found that there was very little accessible transportation, so we decided to rent a car for sightseeing. She was always willing to do anything to assist me and decided that she would transfer me into the front passenger seat and off we went. She drove this small rental car with me in the passenger seat all around the island of Maui. It was a great way for us to see the island, but I did not get out of the car. After driving for several hours, I smelled the strong smell of brake dust. Jamie told me that she also smelled this and that the car was not very responsive to her acceleration. I then noticed that she had never released the emergency brake and we had traveled many miles with it still on! We laughed and chalked it up as another adventure that we would never forget.

During the week in our beautiful hotel room in Maui, I could hear Jamie in the bathroom crying to herself. I went to the door and asked her what was wrong. At first she wouldn't reveal to me why she was crying, and it took me a while to understand her emotions. This was the first time that she truly realized that she had married a quadriplegic who was very dependent upon her and she was scared. This was quite understandable. We were alone in a strange place, far away from friends and family, and there was a recognition that our lives together would often be difficult. She was only 23 years old which was very young to take on these responsibilities. I was 27 and happy to be married but also afraid that maybe I should have given her more time to better understand what she was committing to. I guess a honeymoon is supposed to be a time when a young married couple can be alone together romantically and also get to truly start their lives together. Our honeymoon was a beautiful trip but it was also a time of realization that was scary for both of us. She had committed to be with me despite the many difficulties that we would certainly face. I questioned if it was fair of me to ask her to be in this position with so many responsibilities and future concerns as my wife. Is life fair? Jamie and I decided that we would make the most of our lives together, and the future would be fair to us if we were optimistic and could always lean on each other.

Pursuing Employment

Now that I had my Master's degree, it was time to leave the world of academia and enter the real world of paid employment. Throughout my graduate work I was motivated to get out into the work world but was always concerned that no one would want to hire somebody with a severe disability like mine. My physical limitations required that I would at times need the assistance of people around me, and I was not sure where I would be able to fit in.

I had made a positive impression with the administrators at the Harmarville Rehabilitation Center where I had completed my residency. At the time of my graduation, Mr. Lacey and Bob Henger, who was one of the facility's vice presidents, offered me the opportunity to serve as the Executive Director of a vocational rehabilitation agency that had not been started yet. Grant monies of $250,000 had been approved through the state of Pennsylvania for this pilot project that was intended to create job opportunities and competitive employment for individuals with severe disabilities. The grant was for a two-year period and Harmarville had been awarded this money to serve the southwestern region of Pennsylvania. The state initiative was to test a concept called "supported employment" where job coaches provide direct, one-on-one teaching and support to individuals with severe developmental and physical disabilities or mental health issues so they can work in regular business settings and not in sheltered employment. I was not familiar with this concept and type of work, but when it was presented to me it sounded interesting and I was up for the challenge.

I was being given the opportunity to start a business from scratch, including finding a convenient site for setting up an office, purchasing all necessary furniture and equipment, recruiting and hiring staff, setting up the statistical and financial reporting systems and reporting to an impressive Board of Directors. I knew that I would be able to staff the agency with an administrative secretary who would be able to assist me in clerical functions but also with personal issues related to my disability. I accepted the challenge and began to use my education and intuition in creating this new business that we named Competitive Employment Opportunities or CEO. Although I had the desire to work in a more traditional inpatient or medical facility, I realized that this would give me great experience and an opportunity to further prove my abilities to Harmarville and, ultimately, to myself. The grant money awarded by the state was for two years. I figured that after this period of time I should have this business up and operating successfully, and with this experience on my resume, could search for new endeavors.

In the hiring of new staff, I first approached my good friend BJ Rayburg to work as one of the job coaches. BJ was a very outgoing person and his personality and gift of gab made him a perfect fit to approach employers as we would try to find job opportunities for our clients. He had previous experience in vocational rehabilitation, and I would come to rely upon his insight to deal with this supported employment concept. BJ had been a friend of mine since high school and remained very loyal to me after I'd had my accident. I was happy to be able to offer him a job because of our friendship but mostly because I knew that he had the abilities to do well. I continued interviewing for several vacant positions and made one hire that I will always be thankful for. Jim Shanahan was a young man with moderate cerebral palsy who did not have much experience but had proper formal education in this field. His communication skills were good, even though his response was sometimes delayed when speaking, and his smile was captivating. Initially, I was concerned about hiring him because of his disability and his lack of experience. Imagine! He was in the same situation that I had been in prior to starting this business. I had a physical disability with limited work experience and was hoping for an opportunity to prove myself. When first meeting Jim, I could see that he was motivated to be given this opportunity and working with others with disabilities was perfect for him. After much consideration, I decided that he was the right candidate for me to choose. Years later, he went on to be promoted into the same position that I had held as Executive Director. This is a success story that I am very proud to have been part of because I was willing and able to give him a start and an opportunity to prove himself.

In my first job, I began to understand my physical limitations and how I could get things done at work by utilizing the staff around me. I often delegated tasks that required physical manipulation to those who had the ability and I learned to adapt tasks that I needed to do. This was in the late 1980s and computers on everyone's desks were not standard. I relied upon my telephone with a speakerphone attachment for my routine form of communication. I dictated written reports and gave the cassette tapes to my secretary for transcription. It was a much slower method of completing tasks compared to the advanced technology used today.

I had my difficulties in learning how to manage people in those first two years at CEO. I was a bit brash and learned to realize that even though I was in charge of this agency, employees will always look for someone to complain to when they are unhappy. I had a few employees who did not like my aggressive push to make the business successful. I was in an industry that was funded by government monies and involved many government employees. I learned that the state agencies that I had to deal with and their bureaucracies were not used to having someone like me who wanted to get things done quickly and efficiently. Jamie knew that I had become dissatisfied with the concept of this pilot project and the increasing demands to travel to Harrisburg often for centralized meetings. Harrisburg, the state capital, sits in the center of the state and is a four-hour drive from Pittsburgh. Near the finish of my second year, my Board of Directors and I decided that I would look for new employment. It was very humbling for me because I knew that I was doing the very best I could, but this position was not the right fit for me. They were appreciative of the startup work that I had done and the many goals I had accomplished, but we all knew that I would be happier working elsewhere.

I began to mail out my resume to inpatient and outpatient rehabilitation facilities. I was optimistic that an employer somewhere would be impressed by my education and experience as an Executive Director and hire me. I wanted to be able to work in a medical setting where I could utilize my graduate education and compete at a faster pace more suited to my personality. This was where my real desire to work had always been ever since my residency days.

Jamie and I decided that since we were both young with nothing except family tying us to the Pittsburgh area, we could move anywhere desirable for new employment. We both liked warm weather so began to search for opportunities in states south of Pennsylvania. It was like shooting in the dark and not knowing exactly where the target was. I knew that it would not be easy for us to relocate, but Jamie was always the optimist and assured me we could do anything that we wanted. I started to get many return letters thanking me for my interest but that no job was available. It was discouraging for me, but I kept sending out my resume and applied the determination that I had learned from my parents and my involvement in wrestling. I knew that if I tried hard enough and didn't give up, an opportunity would eventually come.

I finally got a phone call from Rob Thompson, an administrator at a HealthSouth rehabilitation facility located in Florence, South Carolina. He was being promoted within this young company and was searching for his replacement. We set up a time for him to meet me at my office and discuss the position. After our initial meeting, we both felt that it would be worthwhile for me to make the trip down to Florence to take a look at the facility and get to see the town and local surroundings. I was concerned prior to meeting him that he would be reluctant to employ me because of my physical limitations. To my surprise, his view was the opposite of that. He felt that I could be an excellent role model for the patients of his facility who had physical disabilities.

Jamie and I boarded a plane and headed to South Carolina with much optimism. We landed in Myrtle Beach, then rented an accessible van for the additional 45-minute drive to Florence. I was impressed with the location and was confident that I could manage this facility. After our tour and interview, Mr. Thompson decided that I was quite capable of handling this position and offered me the job on the spot. I told him I would need to discuss this with Jamie but that I was excited about the opportunity. After I returned home, he followed up with me by telephone explaining that although he had made me an offer for the position, the CEO of HealthSouth Corporation, Richard Scrushy, wanted to personally meet with me before finalizing anything. At that time, HealthSouth was a small company that was built on the growth of outpatient facilities but only had four inpatient facilities within the United States. The facility in Florence was one of their first and he wanted to still be involved in the ultimate hiring decision. We flew into Birmingham, Alabama to their corporate headquarters for me to interview and meet with him.

Dealing with an interview is stressful enough but adding the additional burden of making sure that my wheelchair is handled properly during airline flights and accessible transportation is available as needed makes it even more stressful. It was 1989 and this was before ADA, the Americans with Disabilities Act, had been enacted. Accessible transportation could often be very difficult and getting around in strange cities sometimes was impossible. My travel wheelchair allowed me the option of being lifted over high curbs if necessary and transferring into a vehicle without a ramp or lift. This was never ideal but sometimes necessary if I wanted to get where I was going. Fortunately, the flight and arrival to Birmingham went well for Jamie and me and we were able to arrange an accessible van company to pick us up the next morning and take us to the HealthSouth corporate headquarters. Here is where the story gets funny and becomes one of those moments that makes an impression that ultimately changes the direction of your life. While loading into the van, Jamie put on the brakes to the rear wheels of my chair as additional security so I wouldn't move during the ride. It is common for the wheelchair to be locked down to the floor along with a security belt similar to a typical seat belt to prevent any movement.

When we arrived, I was able to get out of the van but my chair seemed very sluggish. We were both nervous for my interview and did not think to release the brakes on my chair. I needed to be on time so I tried not to think about the loud squealing coming from my chair every time I moved. I rolled into the CEO's office hoping to make a great first impression with my best suit and tie along with a very positive attitude. However, I think that the squealing of my wheels every time I moved my chair was extremely distracting and he did not seem very impressed or interested in me. It could have been my disability or maybe the squealing wheelchair that made him decide that I was not the candidate he wanted. It was a strange interview. He spent most of the time talking about himself and making an analogy about his employees needing to have the right appearance and polished shoes. I know that my shoes were polished, but obviously my appearance was not what he wanted. After this meeting and interview I waited to hear back from HealthSouth for several weeks. Then after my numerous attempts to contact them, I received notification that Mr. Scrushy did not feel I was the right person for this position. I was very disappointed but ultimately accepted that this would not have been the best company for me.

I continued my job search for several months and finally got a phone call from a Regional Rehabilitation Hospital located in Hickory, North Carolina. They were looking for a Program Director for their rehabilitation unit and the facility director was impressed that I had done my graduate residency at Harmarville Rehabilitation Center. I never felt it was necessary to describe my physical limitations on my resume, therefore I was concerned about meeting with her without first disclosing my disability. She explained this position to me and in our conversation, I disclosed to her that I had a physical disability and utilized a wheelchair in lieu of ambulation. Without hesitation, she invited me to travel south to Hickory to meet with her and interview with staff. I was relieved to feel that she was still interested in potentially employing me. Once again, Jamie and I packed up and headed south with much hope and optimism for the future.

The Frye Regional Medical Center is located near the foothills of the Blue Ridge Mountains in a fairly small southern town approximately a 45-minute drive northwest of Charlotte. The weather is temperate with mild winters and very little snow. It was what we were looking for — a new home with better weather year-round. The rehabilitation hospital was located within the medical center as a designated unit of this facility. Hickory had developed as one of the largest furniture manufacturing cities in the country and had a reputation as the furniture capital. Much of the employment in this area was provided by the furniture plants and assembly lines. It is a beautiful area with many natural resources and a bit of Southern charm.

I interviewed with Sherry B. Watson, the facility administrator. She was the wife of a preacher from one of the local Baptist churches and seemed to be a very caring, outgoing and friendly person. Also, she did not seem to be concerned about my physical disability and revealed to me that she was an active member of a local group that represented the rights of persons with physical disabilities. I was impressed with her background as a physical therapist and her outlook for the rehabilitation facility. Coincidentally, she also had an opening for a medical social worker and asked if Jamie would be interested in considering this role. Even though Jamie was educated as a rehabilitation counselor, she would be able to fulfill this social worker role under the supervision of a licensed medical social worker. It seemed almost too good to be true! Here was an opportunity for us to work together in this new location. After consideration, we both decided to accept these positions and relocate down south.

Southern Living

I know that our families were happy for us to have this opportunity but were also sad to have us move so far away from them. We were both still fairly young and had been married only two years. Our roots had always been in the Pittsburgh area and it seemed a little hard to leave the place that we had always known as home. I'm sure that Jamie's parents wondered how the two of us would be able to make it on our own as she was my only caretaker. I think that my mother knew that Jamie and I could do it together but still had trouble accepting that I would be so far away. She had dealt with many of the health complications that I had encountered since my accident and knew that, despite my determination to succeed, times could be very trying in the future. My father was still uncertain about my capabilities and feared us being alone. Despite his reservations, he invited both families and all of our friends to a going away dinner at Jenny's, a local restaurant in New Kensington owned by his close friends. It was a warm sendoff to me and Jamie for the start of this new chapter in our lives. We were both a bit fearful of leaving the comfort of our friends and family but had enough confidence in our own abilities to make this move together.

We found an apartment close to the medical center. It seemed like a good temporary location for us. Unfortunately, all of our furniture from our previous condominium in Shadyside took up more room than we had planned and could not fit easily into this smaller space. It was difficult to find a fully-accessible apartment with an accommodating bathroom at that time. We needed to take off the bathroom door so that I could get in, and I was unable to use the bathtub. As always, we made the best of it and knew that after saving a bit of money, we would be able to afford a down payment and look for a house in the area. This was a beautiful area and we figured we would want to stay here for a long time. Living in the apartment was only temporary to us, and we were optimistic that we would be able to find a house to purchase and make our own.

I quickly adapted to my new job and learned the responsibilities of this position much on my own. Sherry gave me some direction but often relied on me to be a self-learner. I was fine with this because I understood the objective and quickly picked up how to accomplish what had to be done. One of my primary responsibilities was to oversee the referrals of new patients and the admission process into our facility. I was able to develop strong working relationships with discharge planners from other local hospitals that resulted in our occupancy rate of this 20-bed unit being regularly full. Jamie was ultimately responsible for preparing patients for discharge and helping them to return either back home or to another level of care. We made a great team, as I was responsible for bringing new patients in and she was responsible for getting discharged patients out.

Living in a small southern town had its drawbacks. We really did not know anyone and had to rely on each other for everything. People who had been born and raised in that area often kept to themselves and didn't openly welcome us into their lives. We were fortunate to meet Don and Martha Hall who both worked with us as speech therapists. They were near our ages and had also relocated from out of the area. Having this in common, we began to bond with them and others who did not have family in the area. On Thanksgiving, we would all get together and have what we called an "orphan dinner" because we sometimes felt lonely not having family near us. We were happy to share these times, though. Our real families would visit whenever possible to make the nine-hour drive south. We enjoyed showing visitors around the area and often made trips west up into the Blue Ridge Mountains to a town called Boone. In the summer, traveling into Boone showcased the beauty of North Carolina and was a temporary relief from the hot temperatures. It was a great time in our lives as Jamie and I experienced a whole new culture while getting to learn more about each other.

We soon bought our first home which was located at the very end of a dead-end street. It was a three-bedroom, two-bath ranch house with the garage and game room on the lower level making them accessible from the lower side. We were ecstatic to find this small but beautiful home with much privacy and a floor plan that could be easily modified for wheelchair accessibility. There were two steps into the front door that we added a ramp onto and only one step into the back door that was easily modified. The master bathroom needed to be remodeled as we removed the bathtub and replaced it with a shower stall that was wheelchair accessible. Jamie and I loved having a home again instead of living in an apartment.

Spending a lot of time together in a house with much room to grow encouraged Jamie to start thinking about expanding our family. I guess that she had never truly accepted that I would be unable to father a child. She believed that there could be many possibilities if we were willing to explore them. We began to read and research about fertility studies that were being conducted at a rehabilitation hospital in Atlanta, Georgia. They had had success in artificial insemination with couples having a spinal cord injured partner. They obtained the semen from a spinal-cord injured male using electrical stimulation and inseminated it into the uterus of his partner. I was a bit skeptical because I had thought that my semen was never going to be fertile. I had always been told since the time of my injury that I could not father a natural child.

Jamie was very positive that we could start a family together by either these fertility studies or possibly adoption. Her optimism was amazing! I began to rethink that maybe, just maybe, this could be true and I could actually be a father. The more that we talked about it and I thought about it, I soon adopted her optimism and decided that we should try to become parents. We knew that these fertility studies could be very expensive but were excited about the possibilities in our future. We decided that we should start to save some money so that we could schedule a trip to Atlanta to begin.

Throughout intercourse over the past several years, neither one of us ever used any type of contraceptives. We never figured that we needed them. I did not have sensation in my penis and therefore was never aware of any type of ejaculation during intercourse. However, there were times that I felt an increase in my heartbeat and muscle spasms throughout my body that were probably a modified form of orgasm. This did not always occur, but it was obvious to us when it did. I honestly felt that we would never be able to get pregnant naturally so enjoyed the intimacy and prayed for the best.

One day Jamie and I were heading to the cafeteria at

work for lunch. I recall a very strong feeling came over me that there really was a good chance we would be able to conceive a baby and I would become a father. This realization was so exciting to think about but still rather hard to believe. The information I had received from the fertility studies along with a strong faith that God was watching over us sparked a true belief in the possibilities though. It was a sensation that made me feel joyful and truly believe that my prayers would come true.

After a great Halloween party at our house, Jamie was *in the mood* and told me she was ovulating. With much passion and love, we were able to create the sensation of an orgasm that I described previously. Soon Jamie missed her regular menstrual period and we both became keenly aware of the possibility but were still skeptical. We purchased a pregnancy kit that she used later in the evening after I had gone to sleep. She came running into the bedroom yelling, "It's blue, it's blue!" while jumping on the bed. She was extremely excited that she was pregnant, but I was skeptical and could not believe that the test was correct. We decided that the next day we would go and purchase another kit and check again. The test results were the same. We were going to be parents!

Becoming Parents

The idea of having a baby was a bit frightening to me. Up to this point, it had always been Jamie and me supporting each other, and I always felt that if something happened to me, she would be able to adapt and move on with her life. She has a college education and is a very intelligent person. I knew that she would miss me, but she could easily support herself. However, bringing a baby into the world who would be dependent on me for financial support, physical development and emotional guidance seemed a bit overwhelming. These were scary thoughts that went through my head while Jamie was pregnant and we prepared for the impending birth. Fortunately, I also knew that Jamie would be a great mother and would always be there for our child even if I was not.

We both continued to work full time at Frye throughout her pregnancy, but at times it was not easy. Jamie amazed me with her tenacity to continue working, maintain a healthy pregnancy and be my only caretaker. In the early months of her pregnancy, she had a very tough time with morning sickness. She would wake up early in the morning to get ready for work, and I could hear her throwing up in the bathroom. Often, the nausea would come over her very quickly. After a brief period, she would be back to normal. It became so common for her in the early months of pregnancy that we just took it as part of our daily routine. I recall many times getting into our van to head to work first thing in the morning and her stopping before backing out of the driveway and getting out so that she could throw up. This would probably take no more than a few minutes; then she would quickly get back into the van and off we would go.

At times we were both in disbelief that she was pregnant and that I was able to father a child, considering all the forecasts that I was given since the onset of my spinal cord injury. I think the excitement and joy that we felt every day knowing that we had been blessed to be parents is what kept us going during difficult times. We knew that it might be tough for us with these added responsibilities, but we were thankful that God gave us a chance to experience parenthood.

On the afternoon of a regular workday, I recall Jamie walking into my office with her small belly protrusion. She closed the door behind her and laid in the middle of the floor on her back claiming that she didn't think that she could do her job much longer. It was a stressful position for her because she was responsible for being a resource to many patients' families and assisting with discharge plans. There was often a high turnover of patients being admitted and discharged, making her job and mine busy and often stressful. I would try to comfort her and wished that I knew how to provide her relief. We knew that there would eventually come a time when she would need to resign from work, but she didn't want to leave yet. She and I relied solely upon each other for both physical and emotional support because we did not have our families near us. Many of our coworkers became our friends and the people that we socialized with away from work. Despite the stress involved for Jamie with maintaining full-time work, I think that she wanted to be around people that she knew at the hospital for as long as possible during her pregnancy. She was always very strong-willed and felt that she could handle the responsibilities of our life and those of becoming a mother.

We were fortunate to have met and worked with great people like Mel Deaton who was the Administrative Assistant to the rehabilitation unit. He was an exceptional employee who would often go out of his way to assist Jamie and me with work and personal issues. When we first bought our house, we wanted to be able to cook outside on a propane grill. We purchased a new grill that came in a box and required much assembly. After opening the box, we realized that this was not going to be a simple assembly and that we really had no one to rely upon to assist us. Jamie was never very handy with tools and although I knew how to use them, I didn't have the physical ability. When Mel heard about this, he readily offered his assistance and showed up at our house with a toolbox in hand. The assembly required several hours of work that he seemed to enjoy, knowing that he was helping us. He never asked for money or any type of remuneration because that is the type of person that Mel was. I will always remember his heavy Southern accent and easy going demeanor which made him such a great coworker and friend. It was people like him that made our experience of working and living in Hickory so worthwhile.

In about her seventh month of pregnancy, we decided that it would be best for Jamie to stop working and begin to focus on herself. She is the type of person who would rather focus on helping other people before helping herself. I assume that's one of the many reasons that she chose to marry me, knowing that she would spend the rest of her life helping me and dealing with my limitations. I continued to work, now as the only wage earner for our soon-to-be growing family. I put my heart and soul into my job every day, and my passion to excel resulted in a bad situation for us. I knew that working in a for-profit hospital meant that patient volume was important because it drove profits. As the program director for this rehabilitation unit, I was given the responsibility of getting patients admitted quickly and efficiently into our facility to keep our census as high as possible. My supervisor Sherry gave me this responsibility, but unfortunately did not give me the authority I needed to carry out these duties.

Several of the clinical staff members were not happy that I continued to keep the unit filled and blamed me for staffing levels that they complained were not adequate. I was not responsible for staffing levels and felt that I was being used as a scapegoat so Sherry could avoid blame. She wanted me and our medical director to keep the beds filled, but avoided conflict with the staff by directing concerns at me rather than supporting my actions. I had other personal differences with Sherry that could not easily be resolved. I felt that I had been doing well in my position, but she did not feel the same way. I soon recognized that this scenario would not change and decided that my voluntary resignation after the baby was born would be the best resolution.

Jamie and I felt that although we enjoyed Hickory, North Carolina, there would be no reason to stay there with a newborn baby when our family was back in Pennsylvania. We decided that we were going to move back to the Pittsburgh area and look for employment there after the baby was born. In retrospect, I realize that this was a rather risky decision because Jamie had already resigned from her job and I was resigning from mine, leaving us with no steady income for a family that included a newborn baby. I had developed much confidence in my abilities though and felt that I would be able to find another position that would fit my needs and where I could be appreciated for my work.

As August 1989 approached, we anticipated the birth of our child. Early one evening, Jamie felt that she was beginning to have contractions and it was time. After speaking with her physician on the phone, she was told to go to bed and not come into the hospital until her water broke. We went to bed that evening knowing that it could happen any time. Jamie's willpower amazed me once again. She woke around midnight telling me that her water had broken and we had better get to the hospital. She proceeded to help me get dressed and transferred me into my wheelchair. I still don't know how she was able to do this while in labor with our baby! We contacted a friend and coworker, Sally Ulin. She was an occupational therapist and wanted to assist us in any way she could. We hurriedly loaded into my van and hastily backed out of our driveway and into the mailbox across the street! Our neighbors, Steve and Penny, would have to wait till later to find out about this mishap. Sally proceeded to drive all of us to the Frye Medical Center which was only a 15-minute trip. When we arrived at the emergency room, the nurse at the registration desk saw me coming in a wheelchair and assumed that I was the future patient. Jamie was walking behind me with Sally's assistance, and we laughed as I redirected the emergency room staff to her attention and not mine. It was a very exciting night as we knew that this was going to be the start of a new stage in our lives.

Jamie was in labor for over seventeen hours. Sally helped tremendously by providing lower-back massages to her for relief of the extensive back pain she was having. I wish that I could have been the person that helped to relieve her pain in that moment. My physical limitations often left me wishing for so much more than I was able to give. It was fantastic that the delivery room allowed me to stay right next to her and hold her hand. I remember her pushing like a disciplined soldier who realized that this was painful but necessary in order to achieve the thing that we wanted the most, to have a baby. After those many difficult hours of labor, I watched our son come into this world and was completely amazed with childbirth. It was the most incredible experience in my life and something that I felt so blessed to have the opportunity to be involved with. In the early afternoon of August 3, 1989, our son Brady Abraham Jacob was born. I couldn't believe that this amazing little person had been created by Jamie and me. I had been able to father a baby after so many years of believing that it would never be true. In the birthing room on that unforgettable afternoon, we all cried with joy, feeling that this truly was a miracle for us. I am happy that Jamie's mother was with us that day and got to experience the beauty of seeing her first grandson born into the world.

Many of our coworkers from the rehabilitation floor continued to call down to the maternity unit, waiting to hear word on Jamie's delivery. News spread throughout the hospital quickly and many friends began to stop down to see our son Brady. We all felt that his birth was very special because everyone knew how much Jamie and I wanted to have a child and the small probability of this actually happening. His birth from a complete quadriplegic father was against all spinal cord research and refuted the prognosis that I was given when injured at the age of 19 years old.

I called my parents back in New Kensington to give them the news they were waiting to hear. I anxiously told my mother, "We have a baby."

She asked, "What is it?"

I replied, "We have a little boy."

I could hear the excitement in her voice as she asked, "What's his name?"

I told her, "Brady Abraham." Abraham was my father's first name. We had selected the name Brady from a roadside billboard that caught our attention months earlier during a trip to Charleston, South Carolina. It was advertising a company called "Brady Construction." We liked the strong sound of it.

She told Dad the news and later revealed to me his eyes began to swell with tears. I never knew my father to cry much, but having his first grandson named after him was overwhelming. It was an honor to name my son after him and carry on our family name. I also began to cry because I was so happy to have this moment in my life where I felt I had contributed to such a beautiful occurrence. My mother and father, who were now on good speaking terms, decided to drive down to Hickory from Pittsburgh as soon as they received word that Brady was born. They completed the nine-hour drive overnight and arrived the next morning at the hospital very tired but excited. Like any proud new grandparents, they wanted to see and hold their grandson. I recall my father being exhausted but in a state of euphoria that made me so happy. We took a photo as he held Brady in his arms, sat back on a couch and peacefully fell asleep with him. I was able to give to him the one thing in his life that he did not have, a grandson.

When we returned home, Jamie and I quickly learned how having a baby completely changes your lives. She stayed at home to care for Brady and I continued to work at Frye while looking for job opportunities in the Pittsburgh area. My supervisor, Sherry, knew that I was looking for a new job, but I did not plan to write my resignation letter until I could find new employment. Now with a wife and son dependent upon me, I knew that it was essential for me to find a good job so we could return back home to Pittsburgh.

Hurricane Hugo

I honestly believe that there are events in everyone's life that are meant to be and will shape their future. I don't know whether God intends this as a way to better us, challenge us or strengthen us, but I follow the philosophy that everything that happens was meant to be. It was in mid-September that weather forecasts predicted that a hurricane was growing in the Atlantic Ocean and was expected to strike Charleston, South Carolina. This was hurricane season in the South, but typically these types of storms never came as far north and inland as Hickory. It was expected that Hurricane Hugo would start on land in South Carolina and die out to a tropical storm by the time it traveled north into central North Carolina where we were located. We knew that a storm was coming from the south but did not expect much damage in our area. Brady was only six weeks old and seemed to enjoy any kind of excitement that would give him an excuse to stay awake. As the skies started to darken and the wind became powerful, I began to fear the worst and recognize that this storm may not weaken as initially expected. I recall seeing Jamie holding Brady in her arms standing in front of the large front window in our family room. I warned her to get away from the window as we could see trees blowing side to side and hear the sound of strong rain pelting off of the roof. We decided to retreat into a back room that did not have a large window in case the storm continued to worsen. Here we were in the midst of a hurricane with a newborn baby, no family or support system around us, and limited income due to Jamie no longer working and me on the verge of a pressured resignation. It was not a very comforting feeling and it was at that point that I knew we needed to quickly make a change in our lives and pursue our return back home to Pennsylvania even before I secured another position.

After many hours of the storm, we lost our electricity and had no light or heating source available in the house. We finally went to bed when the wind started to die down, expecting that in the morning all would be well. Waking up the next day, we were shocked to look outside and see what looked like a war zone in our front yard and neighborhood. Many trees had been blown over and there were electric lines laying down on the ground. Although the heart and strength of Hurricane Hugo had struck Charleston first, it unexpectedly still maintained its power as it traveled north into our area. The downed power lines caused much chaos for us. I now had no way of recharging my electric wheelchair which we typically plugged in every evening. Without this electricity, my chair battery would go dead and

I would have no way to motor around. We also had electric heating for the house along with an electric oven for cooking. This meant that Jamie was unable to prepare bottles for Brady. As new parents, we learned that babies are not very patient when it comes to feeding time, and they are also very finicky about the temperature of their milk. In addition, the storm left us with an overcast sky that dropped the temperature significantly so that we were not comfortable without a heater. We were very concerned that a cold house would be unhealthy for our new son.

After spending one night in our house trying to make the best of this situation, we decided it was necessary to find a place with electricity and heat. Unfortunately, all of the hotel rooms in Hickory were filled since many people were facing the same issues. We were able to find a hotel room in a neighboring town about 45 minutes away. Off we went with a bag full of empty baby bottles, my battery recharger and a small suitcase of clothes mostly consisting of baby items. I often recall this as a very low point in our lives. We were facing so many challenges and had no one around to help us. Six weeks prior to this we were on top of the world with the birth of Brady and the excitement of what the future held. It was ironic that such a short time later we would be in such a dismal situation and feeling the desperation in our lives with no future employment, no electricity and no heat in our home.

After several days, electricity was restored and debris from the storm was cleared from our neighborhood to make roads easily passable. We had endured a difficult event and were able to grow stronger as a result of it. Jamie and I now knew it was time to move on from our time and life in Hickory and return home with our new son. Hurricane Hugo was a life-changing event for us for many reasons, and ultimately it shaped Brady's life.

Heading North

I resigned from my position and we put our house up for sale and headed back north to search for work and start a new chapter in our lives. My father had recently built a beautiful ranch-style home in New Kensington that was wheelchair-accessible. He offered to let us move in with him and my brother, Tony. He had designed the house for my accessibility, but I don't think he expected me to be living there so soon. Jamie and I figured that living there would give us an opportunity to begin job searching in the Pittsburgh area without incurring the expense of an apartment. My father had even offered me a position with his own business. In 1983, he had started his own physical therapy private practice and had been slowly growing this business over the past six years. Westmoreland Armstrong Physical Therapy was located in Leechburg, PA and had a small support staff along with one other physical therapist to operate the outpatient facility and provide contracted service to a local nursing home. I felt that my father had offered me a position that he truly didn't need to have filled but wanted to give me an opportunity that he felt I might not receive elsewhere.

My father always cared very much about me, and after my spinal cord injury he became deeply concerned that my future would be extremely difficult. He knew from working previously with spinal cord injured patients that there were going to be many challenges and difficult situations to deal with. He always encouraged me to pursue further education, but I felt that he doubted I would ever be able to maintain substantial employment and ultimately make it on my own. I can understand why he would feel this way, but I have always felt that my determination would allow me to be successful if I just worked hard enough. I had learned this work ethic from my father, and ironically I now felt that I needed to prove it to him. I had always strived to make my parents proud of me. It was a strong motivator for me. I decided to turn down a good job offer from my father so that I could prove to him and myself that I could succeed on my own despite my disability.

After a few months of job searching, I was fortunate to meet with Toby Kennerdell who was a Vice President at the Suburban General Hospital located in Bellevue, PA. He was searching for a Director of Rehabilitation Services and called me in for an interview. He had received my resume previously and was impressed with my work history. I had never met Toby prior to this but connected with him right from the start. He had graduated from a high school near mine and I felt as if I had somehow known him in the past. He was an easygoing guy who I felt comfortable with because I sensed that he was able to look past my obvious disability and see my capabilities. As previously indicated, I was always very concerned that my disability and use of an electric wheelchair would scare off employers and make my hiring less probable. This was the case with many interviews that I had where the interviewer spoke more about himself and never really wanted to learn more about me. This was not my experience with Toby, and I felt positive about our meeting and his willingness to hire me.

Shortly after our interview, I received a call from Toby and was offered the job. I was ecstatic because the salary was good and it was a perfect job situation for me at that point in my life. Suburban General Hospital was only a 45-minute drive from our families and was a community hospital that had a great need for their rehabilitation department to be improved. I knew that I could contribute much to this department and prove my value to the hospital. The department lacked strong management and many of the hospital's orthopedic surgeons did not refer their patients for on-site physical therapy but instead referred to outside providers. I accepted the position. I didn't realize how fortunate I was at the time to have crossed paths with Toby. I feel that God presented me with this opportunity and I was intuitive enough to take advantage of it.

In the late fall of 1989, Jamie, Brady and I moved into an apartment complex in the North Hills of Pittsburgh. This small apartment was only a 15-minute drive to my new employer and was located near many stores and conveniences. As a new mother, Jamie was always finding a need to shop and this location was ideal for her. We had figured that we would eventually look for a house in that area but wanted to first find stability in my job and figure out what community would be the best location for us. Jamie continued to be the only person who would assist me at home with my personal needs, but now with a baby to care for, I needed to find someone else that could drive me to work every day. It was not sensible to try to get all of us prepared in the morning and take Brady out into the inclement weather. A cold Pittsburgh winter was on its way, and we knew that it would be necessary for me to not rely upon Jamie for this daily responsibility.

My search for a driver led me to get to know Jamie's first cousin, Cindy Nelson. She lived in the area and was looking for part-time employment. When we ultimately decided to move back to Pittsburgh from North Carolina, it was because of our desire to be closer to our family support system. Having Cindy come into our lives at that time was a perfect example of this. I now had a good job, assistance with transportation, and a nice apartment that suited our needs well. Life was looking positive for us.

Moving back to Pittsburgh also meant adjusting to the colder weather that we had grown up in but had easily forgotten while living in the milder North Carolina climate. One Saturday afternoon while we were out shopping at the mall with Brady, a fast-moving snowstorm delivered a foot of snow. It was a heavy snow that came very quickly, and we were happy when we returned to our apartment complex, having feared that we may have gotten stuck out on a roadway. When we pulled into our parking lot, it was obvious that no one had been around to clear any of the fallen snow yet. The plow crew would wait until no more snow was falling before they started their work. This meant that nearly a foot of heavy fresh snow covered my parking space and the 150-foot walkway that separated us from the front doorway. My full-size van had a lift on the side that could get me easily out of the van but when it reached the ground level, I was confronted with a very difficult obstacle. My electric wheelchair would easily push through several inches of snow but a full foot was too much. The temperature was frigid so I attempted to plow through it and make my way onto the sidewalk. Despite my valiant attempts, I found myself stuck in the snow with my wheels spinning with no traction. The snow was continuing to fall and I began to look around to see if there was anyone in the area that might be able to help me push my way through the snow.

Jamie had gotten out of the van to try to push me, but she was not strong enough to move me in such deep snow. I told her that I would sit there while she took Brady into the warm apartment and could try to find someone to help. I assumed that she would be able to quickly get Brady settled and locate someone in a nearby apartment. As I sat in the parking lot with snow falling on my head and the frigid cold wind blowing in my face, I began to question my logic for getting out of the van and attempting to traverse the snow-covered walkway. I started to wonder how long it would be before Jamie would return and I could get rescued from this situation. Unfortunately, she was not able to readily find somebody and I waited nearly ten minutes before she came back with a willing volunteer. They pushed me through the snow and out of the frigid weather. I was happy to see Brady safe in the apartment and I realized that having a young baby during these winter months was not going to be easy.

Before my injury, I enjoyed lots of outdoor activities like snow skiing and ice skating. These cold Northern winters affected me drastically after my accident because living with a spinal cord injury affects my ability to stay warm. Not having the ability to get up and increase my circulation with regular movement or increased activity has caused me to hate the cold and try to avoid it whenever possible. At first I didn't recognize how badly the cold would affect me, but after several winters I learned that colder weather was no longer sensible for me. Every winter I would catch a cold which eventually would affect my lungs and ability to breathe normally. My C5 spinal cord injury paralyzed the intercostal muscles in my chest. These are the muscles that are in between each rib and assist in regular breathing and coughing to remove any mucus in the lungs. When I develop a cold and it settles into my lungs, I have difficulty breathing and have been hospitalized many times due to risk of pneumonia. This is a serious condition for anyone, but even more serious for a quadriplegic who has no control over his intercostal muscles and the ability to cough phlegm out of his lungs.

Many times these illnesses left me wheezing for air and often completely wiped out. When phlegm would build up in my chest, I could hear the rattling and it would keep me awake at night as I lay on my side. Trying to expel phlegm without having the use of intercostal muscles is tiring and sometimes impossible. Intravenous antibiotics were the primary defense used to kill the infection along with medicated breathing treatments to dilute the phlegm and mucus in my chest. During many nights when I had gotten very sick, I would lay awake in bed alone with my thoughts and wondered why God kept me alive and prolonged my agony. In spite of this, I was fortunate that I had people in my life that never gave up on me. I recognized that I had a lot to live for and never wanted to give up on them. Jamie learned how to care for me during these times of sickness and would always be there. She was my driving force and I counted on her because I knew I could.

I came to realize that I needed to be very careful about letting myself get too cold and putting myself in a position where I could get sick and develop pneumonia. I began to avoid going outside in the winter for any prolonged period of time. I have always continued to work but in the winter months do not do any activities outside. These bouts with pneumonia could be very dangerous for me, and I learned to avoid getting sick at all costs.

In spite of the trying winters, Jamie, Brady and I had settled into life in southwestern Pennsylvania, and my job position at Suburban General Hospital was going well. I had a good working relationship with my boss because he recognized the positive outcomes that I had accomplished in my role as director of rehabilitation services. After having worked in this position for a year, Jamie and I decided that we would look for a house, possibly in the neighborhoods near the hospital. We began searching for a ranch house with a flat driveway and yard.

This area of Pittsburgh where we were located was called the North Hills. When searching for a house with our expectations, we learned why it was called the North Hills. In southwestern Pennsylvania there are many hills and rivers that make finding flat land quite difficult. We began working with a realtor, looking on weekends for an ideal setting that might suit my accessibility needs and those of my young family. Much to our disappointment, we were not able to find a suitable home in this area within our price range and started to consider other options. Our realtor suggested that if we traveled north into Cranberry Township in Butler County we might be able to find a flat piece of property where we could build a new accessible house. Cranberry Township was a growing community because a new highway, Route 279, had been built that allowed quick and easy access into Pittsburgh from the North. A trip from this area to the hospital was only a 25-minute commute. I figured that I could hire a driver to take me back and forth to the hospital on workdays and that Jamie and I could still easily access many other parts of the area.

We found a flat, one-third acre piece of property at the end of a cul-de-sac in a new development. After many months of searching, this seemed like an ideal place to build a home that would meet all of our requirements and was located in a growing area with many other young families.

We contracted with a builder and started the process of selecting a house design that was wheelchair accessible and fit the existing property guidelines. We started building in the fall of 1990, hoping for completion as quickly as possible. Living in a small apartment with a toddler was not very comfortable. It was difficult for us to get to the house site on weekdays during construction because of my work schedule. We would drive to Cranberry Township on weekends to try to see the progress as best as possible, but any worksite that is unfinished is often difficult to traverse.

We moved into our new house in February 1991 in the midst of a cold winter. We were anxious and happy to move out of our apartment and have a new home for our family. I guess the happiness and excitement of getting a new home resulted in Jamie and me conceiving another baby! I had always thought when we conceived Brady that it was a one-time miracle, and I never imagined that it would happen again. As I was told, lightning never strikes twice in the same place. Jamie was always the optimist who believed I could father children and never resorted to using any contraception, though. I was amazed that we had done it again! I actually think that there were doubts from others about Jamie and me conceiving Brady naturally without utilizing a sperm donor or some other type of assistance. Getting pregnant with Maria ended any doubts that we were able to conceive children naturally and squelched any thoughts that Brady was not my natural son.

Brady was a kid who would amaze us with his endless energy and desire to not want to sleep at night. He was colicky as an infant, always keeping us up. As he grew into a toddler, he became more determined to keep us up beyond our capabilities. I loved him but never imagined how difficult having a child like him would be. It made me fearful that we would be having a second child with as much energy as Brady.

Jamie was the one who did all of the physical work with our kids, and I often had to put their interests ahead of mine and wait for her assistance. This may seem normal in any parenting relationship, but as a quadriplegic I often had many needs that I could not address on my own. I would try to help her in any way possible, even if it meant delaying a necessity for myself. One of my favorite things as a new father was feeding a bottle to Brady. Jamie would place a pillow on my lap and then let him lay on top of it while I held the bottle. Brady would look up at me with his big, beautiful brown eyes and I would talk to him hoping that he would be able to connect with my voice and my face. This was the time when I felt that I was contributing to his care and helping Jamie. Such a small thing may not seem like much to anyone else, with my physical limitations, it meant the world to be able to hold him on my lap and realize what Jamie and I had created.

I often tried to find ways to connect with Brady as a father. I was fearful that he would see me differently because of my disability and not have the same respect or love for me as other sons did for their fathers. I was very physically active prior to my spinal cord injury and I guess I felt that I would need to be physically active with him. I always wanted to be that father that could go out in the backyard and catch baseball with him or wrestle with him on the living room floor. As a young guy, I envisioned that this would be the relationship that I had with my son. I loved having him around me but often wished that I could do so much more with him. I envied fathers who could become friends with their sons through sports and other physical activities. I often tried to explain these feelings to Jamie, but I think that she had difficulty understanding the bonding between a father and son.

It made me feel good to be active with Brady and wanted him to know that even though I had a physical disability, I would always be there to support him emotionally. I liked to find ways that I could contribute physically to our family and not just as a financial resource. I know that my role was to be the breadwinner but wanted to be more than just that.

On an early summer day I decided to take almost-two-year-old Brady out for a walk in our new neighborhood. It was an opportunity for us to do something together and for me to help relieve Jamie of her constant duties as a young, pregnant mother. We lived on the end of a cul-de-sac and there was not much traffic in this neighborhood of new families. He walked next to me as I rolled down the street to the corner where a new house was being built. The cinder block foundation had been laid, but the dirt around the house had not been leveled yet. This left about a four-foot ravine all around the house that proved to be very tempting for the curious Brady. He was like a sponge that absorbed everything around him and often his curiosity would get him into trouble. As we approached the house, I warned him to not get too close to the ravine but I was unable to physically pull him back. He proceeded to try and see what was at the bottom of the hole. Much to my dismay, as he leaned over to look forward, he fell headfirst into the hole and was wedged upside down between the cinder block foundation and the dirt soil. He started to scream and cry and I quickly realized that I had no way to pull him out as his feet were the only part of his body that I could see. I became very scared because I did not know if he was hurt and in danger. I tried to calm him down by telling him that I was going to go get help, but I don't think that he could hear me over his screaming. It was a horrible feeling, not being able to help him. This was the first time that I had ever experienced this type of situation. I was alone with Brady and I was responsible for his safety.

As quickly as I could, I turned around and put my electric chair into the fastest speed that I had. I zoomed back up the road leaving Brady alone, screaming and trapped upside down in this ravine. My heart was racing as I tried to get back to my house for help from Jamie. I was yelling as loud as I could as I rolled up the street, but my chair seemed like it was only crawling. As I finally got near our house, the front door opened. Jamie came running out, knowing that something was wrong when she saw me alone without Brady. I quickly told her that he had fallen into a hole, and without any hesitation, she began to run down the road, cutting through a connecting field as fast as she could. Her speed was inhibited because she was six months pregnant and barefoot. She could hear him screaming and headed directly to the house site on the corner. Despite her condition, she raced much faster than I could travel and beat me to the site. When she arrived, she pulled him up by his ankles and much to our relief, he was okay. He had scratched up his head and gotten quite dirty, but fortunately there was no serious damage.

As Jamie carried him back to the house, I realized that this situation would have never occurred if I was not disabled. I would have been able to easily divert him away from any danger prior to it happening, and I would have been able to easily rescue him myself, if needed. What would have happened if the hole he fell into was deeper and he was seriously injured? How would I have ever forgiven myself if I had allowed him to be permanently hurt? I learned that day that I would need to be much more cautious with my children as I was now the protector and not the one being protected.

Despite an occasional mishap, it was a fantastic time in our lives. I had a job that I enjoyed going to every day, a beautiful pregnant wife at home, a healthy two-year-old son and now an accessible new house of our own. I felt like I had everything that I had worked so hard for. I was living the American dream.

Changing It All

In early summer of 1991, Jamie and I invited my father and his girlfriend, Nancy Skulos, to our new house for the first time. Brady was almost two years old and Jamie was pregnant with Maria. I felt that this was the first time in my life that I had achieved a lifestyle that my parents would be proud of. We had dinner together that day and Jamie and I had an opportunity to get to know Nancy a little better. Dad had been seeing her for less than a year, and we didn't really know much about her. I could see that my father was happy with her and that made me happy. He had had a difficult time with the separation and divorce from my mother which had left him very sad and lonely for many years.

On that afternoon as they talked alone, Nancy revealed to Jamie that my father was extremely proud of me. It was a beautiful day that I will fondly remember, as I finally felt that my father realized I had accomplished much on my own. I highly valued making my parents proud and had always been worried that I would not. I guess it was knowing how much they loved me even despite all the problems that our family had during my years growing up. In my heart I had always known that my father was proud of me, but it was wonderful to hear it.

Several weeks later, while at home on the evening of July 8, 1991, I received a phone call from a good friend of mine. He gave me the shocking news that dad had had a heart attack and died that day. It was a hot summer day and he had decided to go jogging after finishing work. He went to a local high school track that he and I had run on for many years and collapsed in a grassy area near the track. He was found later by another friend of mine who said Dad had been lying peacefully.

I was stunned by this news but should probably have seen it coming. Dad had already had a minor heart attack six months earlier and was told by his physician that he would need to change his lifestyle and reduce his stressful activities, especially since he was an insulin-dependent diabetic. I knew that he would have difficulty slowing down his work but tried to convince him that he should take time away to relax. Nancy and he had talked about taking a trip to the Greek islands. This is the type of trip that my father had never taken before, and I was happy to think that he would enjoy it. He had finally hired another physical therapist who would be able to provide coverage for treatment of his patients while he was away. He had worked so hard all of his life, and I wanted him to have a chance to enjoy the fruits of his labor.

Sadly, at the age of 63 he passed from this world, leaving behind a legacy that shaped my life.

My father had cared very deeply for me and must have decided due to my disability that I would be the sole benefactor of his business and personal assets. I know that he cared for my siblings, but they had distanced themselves from him, and I think that he felt they were all perfectly healthy and capable of caring for themselves. In his will there was no mention of my siblings or explanation of his intentions. His attorney and executor explained to me that Dad had wanted me to have the house that he had built to be completely wheelchair accessible and to take over his business, as he knew my education and work experience could be well-utilized in this capacity. I decided that I would give each of my siblings something from his estate because I felt it was fair to do so. I actually wished that he had delineated in his will something to give to each of us regardless of its value so that I would not feel the burden and responsibility of dividing his assets. It was extremely hard for me and created some dissension and animosity amongst us, even though I explained that Dad did not list any of them as benefactors.

With the loss of my father and the inheritance of his small business, I was now faced with one of the most important decisions of my life. Should I pursue running this business on my own or simply try to sell it to an interested buyer? The business was not very large; it had eight regular employees. My father was the primary clinician in this practice and generated most of the income. Without him, it would be essential to recruit others to fill in for the many roles that he had fulfilled. At that time, the recruitment of licensed physical therapists was difficult because there was a shortage of staffing, especially those interested in working with geriatric patients. I had never managed a private practice or knew the regulations involved with this type of Medicare certification. I had served as a member of his advisory board, but this had exposed me to only a limited amount of information regarding the business as a whole.

I was at a crossroads in my life and I was truly questioning which way to head. I had to truly soul search and assess where I was at that time in my life. I was married and had started a family with a son and another child soon on the way. Jamie was a stay-at-home mom and we all relied upon my income from my position with Suburban General Hospital. It was a stable job that I enjoyed and my salary was adequate for our needs. It seemed obvious to me that leaving the position that I was in would be risky for my future income and the stability of my growing family. However, I knew that this was a once-in-a-lifetime opportunity that I would never get again. I thought back to the many times in the past when I had been turned down for positions that I was well qualified for due to my physical disability. This was an opportunity for which I did not need to interview. I think my father knew that I had the capabilities to do it and had started his business hoping that I could be successful on my own. I had much conversation with Jamie regarding taking over the business. She also felt that it was an opportunity for not just me, but for all of us.

After his funeral, I notified my current boss and employer that I would be resigning my position within one month. I knew that I had obligations with this job and didn't want to leave my department without assisting with a transition. However, it was imperative that I begin immediately to keep my dad's business together and this meant being there on-site as soon as possible. During the early 1990s, personal computers were limited and there was no such thing as the internet. Over the next month, I worked at the hospital throughout the day and on many evenings traveled to Leechburg to keep track of the daily operations. Jamie and I would load Brady into our van and make the nearly one-hour trip from our new house in Cranberry Township. It was very helpful that Jamie's sister, Barbara Gray, had been my dad's assistant and was able to keep the office running while I made my transition into this business. Despite her assistance, it was scary at times because I often felt that I had very limited guidance in this entrepreneurial role. My father wasn't there and none of the other employees could fill his role or independently manage the business. However, it was very exciting to now have the autonomy to run a business of my own and no longer need to answer to a higher level. No one but me would judge my capabilities and be concerned about my physical disability. It was the best of times; it was the worst of times.

I began to assess the strengths and weaknesses of the business and determined that it would be necessary to expand locations and diversify services in order to remain stable into the future. I had bigger dreams and decided to start opening additional outpatient facilities in local surrounding communities duplicating what had already been started in Leechburg. My experiences at Suburban General Hospital lent well to this work as I knew how to recruit valued employees and manage a professional staff. I used these experiences, along with my graduate school education, to begin growing the business. Dad had provided me with a solid foundation and now I could try to create a larger entity that could survive without him.

I was confident that I needed to make changes within the company that would result in future growth and position us for long-term success. However, I continued to have reservations about my efforts because I was concerned that my father would not have been in agreement with my decisions. I secretly worried that I would make mistakes that might be detrimental to everyone involved and ruin the hard work that he had put into starting this business. It was not until one night that I had a very enlightening dream. In the dream I was speaking with my father. With concern I asked him, "Dad, are you proud of the way that I am running your company"? His answer to me was very surprising and completely changed my direction for the future. He simply said to me, "Son, it's not my company anymore." That was all he said, but it was enough to wake me in tears. His voice and face were so real in that dream that I truly felt he was speaking to me once again. I guess I had expected him to say that he was alright with how I was doing things or to give me advice on my work. I felt relieved from the burden that my father would not have approved of my work. Now I knew that he was no longer worried about the company and that it was in my hands.

Jamie and I put our new home up for sale and moved back to New Kensington to live in my father's accessible house. We felt that it would have been very inconvenient for us to stay in Cranberry and commute daily to Leechburg. Also, with Jamie being pregnant we realized that it would be helpful to be closer to her parents and my family for support. My brother Tony continued to live in the house in the downstairs game room as he had lived with my father previously. He had a full-time job but did not have the means to own his own home at that time. Also, although he and my father were strained, I felt that they had provided each other with companionship being in the same household. After he lived with me and my family for several months, I assisted Tony with a down payment so that he could purchase his own house. It had become awkward at times having Tony in the basement because Jamie and I were used to having our own home and space. I always loved my brother and wanted to help him in his life but realized that he had to help himself first.

It was a beautiful ranch-style house with many wheelchair accessible features that my father had thoughtfully included. We felt blessed that we had this house that was only fifteen minutes away from my new job and business. We settled into the neighborhood and made the house our own. After having made numerous moves to different homes over the past few years, Jamie and I finally felt settled and ready to raise our son and future daughter.

The Most Beautiful Face I Ever Saw

Jamie always amazed me when she was pregnant because she never slowed down, regardless of any physical limitations. On a very cold night at the start of 1992, she was admitted to our local community hospital for the birth of our daughter. We were both anxious with the expectation of seeing this baby that she had carried for the last nine months. The delivery room at this hospital was more restrictive than what we had experienced with the birth of Brady in North Carolina. They did not permit me to stay close to Jamie and instead limited me to stay just inside the doorway of the delivery room. Jamie's sister Barb and I stood there watching Maria Elise come into this world. I could see the doctor standing below Jamie as she was lying on the delivery table and remembered him telling her to push. As she bore down, it seemed like it was going to be a much quicker and easier delivery than the first one we had experienced with Brady.

Suddenly, the doctor commanded for her to stop and I sensed that there was a problem. The umbilical cord had been wrapped around the baby's neck and it was starting to strangle her. He quickly began to cut the umbilical cord in order to release the pressure from her neck. After cutting through the cord, he directed Jamie to push again. Within seconds, Maria entered our world and I could see her starting to cry as she was held up. As I watched this miracle happen, I wished that I could see her closer but the nurse wanted to clean her first. I anxiously waited in the doorway like a kid waiting for Christmas morning to come.

When she was finally placed in Jamie's arms, I was able to get close enough to see her. In that moment, I looked at the most beautiful little face I have ever seen! She had a tuft of light brown hair on her head along with gorgeous blue eyes. Jamie asked me if I thought she was pretty, and I told her that she was beautiful. I fell in love with that face at first sight. This birth was very different than Brady's because I was not as unknowing or fearful of what to expect. He had seemed to be so much more traumatized by the long labor period, but Maria accepted coming into this world more graciously. I felt like the luckiest man in the world!

Initially, I was afraid to have a daughter because I never thought that I would know how to raise her or how to be a father to a girl. I guess I was fearful that my daughter would grow up without a strong male figure involved in her developmental years because of my disability. Having a son seemed like second nature to me because I always figured that I would be able to easily relate to him as a male and would know what boys like to do as he grew up. Having a daughter and trying to understand the mind of a young girl made me worry. My own father never really related to my sisters and I knew that I didn't want to be like that with Maria. He loved my sisters but never spent much time with them or showed them outward affection. I knew that they had grown up missing this attention, and it had an adverse effect on their development in life.

In 1993, Jamie and I decided that, although we were living in the wheelchair-accessible house my father had built, we wanted to build our own house with the features that we desired. Our current house did not have a large backyard and we wanted room for our kids to be able to play outside while they grew up. We had also heard that the local school district had plans to start busing elementary school kids from our neighborhood into a rougher area and we were not in favor of this. From previous experiences in searching for a home in the North Hills, we knew that it was difficult to find an existing house that was wheelchair accessible. During our search, we found an empty, one-acre lot for sale in Lower Burrell, a neighboring town to New Kensington. It was mostly flat and was one of the last plots left in a new, upscale neighborhood named Indian Fields. It seemed ideal for our plans because the property was private and located in a well-respected school district.

I was having success in my work and felt comfortable enough financially to build a new house. We decided that it would be sensible to hire Emery Szalai, an architect, to assist us with plans for a wheelchair-accessible home. I wanted to make sure that there would be many features of this home that would fulfill my special needs, Jamie's desires and the demands of our two small children so we could finally settle in. Emery was an excellent person for us to work with. He had extensive experience designing commercial buildings and was now semi-retired and starting to work on private homes. In addition, his calm personality made it very easy for us to work with him and, over time, become friends.

I would go out of my way to pay attention to Maria whenever possible. I often read her children's books that Jamie had bought and I really enjoyed being the focus of her attention. She sometimes asked me to play Barbie dolls with her. I didn't know how to play dolls with a girl because this is something that I had never done in my life. How was I supposed to do this? Regardless of my inexperience, I wanted to spend time with her and made every attempt I could.

She had a full collection of Barbie and Ken dolls, clothes, houses and even play cars. I would pretend to be Ken and go on fictitious dates with Barbie. I would disguise my voice in a deep tone and say things that I thought a guy doll would say to an attractive girl. Things like, "Hi Barbie, do you want to go on a date?" Maria would get agitated with me and tell me, "Daddy, don't do that voice!" I would just laugh out loud and play on, showing up in the red Corvette convertible that was part of Maria's collection. I guess I found out that playing dolls really wasn't that hard; it only required you to live out your fantasies.

I never imagined that these play dates would someday become reality. Maria often told us as a young girl that she wanted to eventually live in Ohio. We questioned her, "Why Ohio?" After graduating from high school, she chose the University of Cincinnati to start her college life. This is where she met her real-life Ken doll, Grant Mallory. He was that young suitor who seemed at a loss for words at first but became the love of her life. They dated throughout her college years and eventually married. They have now settled in Cincinnati, Ohio and are very happy together.

Another one of my favorite memories with Maria was playing a game called "Pretty Pretty Princess". This game involved many pieces of jewelry (crown, earrings, necklaces, rings) and spinning a wheel to determine which player would wear these different pieces. The winner was determined by who finally was completely dressed in this jewelry. Now, understand that I was never a person to wear any jewelry and the idea of being covered in it was comical. She would always win the games that we played and loved being the Pretty Pretty Princess wearing the full set of costume jewelry. I often would have to wear the jewelry myself throughout the game but didn't mind because she enjoyed dressing me up, and I enjoyed being the center of her attention.

When Maria started middle school, she had a teacher that gave the class a different math homework problem every evening and required them to try to find the solution. We would sit at the kitchen table together and go over her homework. I loved to assist her with the "problem of the day" because it gave me an opportunity to spend quality time with her, and she counted on me to be her helper. Like any good parent, I wanted her to learn on her own, but I also wanted to assist her in the process. She would come home the next day and let me know if we had come up with the right answer to the problem. Strangely, I took much pride in helping her to present the right answer and began to jokingly refer to this scenario as "Stump the Dad". It felt good to have her rely on me and trust in my assistance. I always thought that maybe I can't do a lot of things physically with her but at least I can use my mental capabilities.

I used the same logic when spending time with Brady. He enjoyed sports, especially those that involved hand-eye coordination. We had enrolled him in Little League

Baseball when he was very young, and he grew to love the sport. At the age of nine he enjoyed pitching for his team and became very good at it. He was picked for an All-Star team that would compete against boys of the same age group from other districts. I had loved to pitch baseball in my youth and I wanted to teach him what I knew. It was very frustrating for me to not be able to physically show him many of these techniques. I knew that I couldn't catch ball with him but decided to do the next best thing.

I bought a pitch back machine which is essentially a framed net that is attached with springs. Throwing into the net forces the ball to spring back and allows the thrower to play catch alone. We set this up in our backyard and he and I spent many hours together as he threw the ball into the net and I instructed him on technique. This practice improved his pitching, but much more importantly to me, it gave us an opportunity to be together as a father and son playing catch. It made me feel like I was important to him, and it helped us to bond. He always thought that I wanted him to practice his pitching but didn't really know that I just wanted to spend time with him and be a father.

My determination to be like every other dad sometimes got me into trouble. One summer afternoon when Maria was nearly two years old, Jamie wanted to go to the store. I told her to take Brady, and I would stay home and watch Maria. We rolled into the backyard with her sitting on my lap to play on the swing set. She sat on my legs facing forward but did not have anything to secure her in place. When we reached the swings, she reached out to grab on and I was unable to hold her from falling off my lap. She fell forward and hit her mouth on one of the wooden ladder steps on the way to the ground. I could feel her falling but was unable to reach out to hold her. I screamed her name when she hit the ground and she started to cry loudly.

When she got up and turned around looking at me there was blood beginning to pour out of her mouth. I was alone with her and never imagined that I would have to deal with this kind of emergency on my own. Through her crying, I instructed her to step up onto my footrest and hold onto my chair so that I could take her somewhere to get help. After she had stepped up and placed her face in my lap, I started to quickly drive my chair to our next-door neighbor's house in hopes that someone would be there. Fortunately, our neighbor Sue answered the door and was able to help us.

I initially thought that all of the blood was because of a cut lip or mouth but found that she had cleanly knocked out one of her eye teeth when hitting the ladder step on her way down. Thankfully, we were able to stop the bleeding and she did not require any stitching. I went back to the swing set later and found her eye tooth completely intact lying on the ground. The impact of knocking out her tooth resulted in trauma to the permanent tooth which eventually grew improperly. This had to be corrected by orthodontic bracing and many visits to the dentist throughout her early teenage years. Even though I know that this was an accident, I have always felt very guilty about letting her fall because I should have been smart enough to know my limitations.

I always tried to involve myself in Brady and Maria's activities, even if I was that embarrassing parent. When Maria was about twelve years old we decided to celebrate her birthday at a local skating arena. We had invited many of her classmates, both boys and girls. While the kids were skating I decided that I would roll out into the rink and have Maria grab onto the back handles of my wheelchair so I could pull her around. When the other kids saw this, they decided that they wanted to also hang on. It resulted in a long train of skaters with me being the locomotive. I didn't realize that Maria was not enjoying this because her arms were getting tired with the weight of everyone being pulled behind her. I laughed as I rolled around the rink, but found I had embarrassed her because I had become the center of attention.

Being a father of two children was a miracle that I had never imagined after sustaining my spinal cord injury. When Brady first came along, it was a true shock and surprise. When Maria came along, it was like lightning striking twice in the same spot. Jamie and I didn't know what being parents would involve but learned quickly that it was extremely demanding of both of us. My disability and limitations required us to be able to raise our children without my physical assistance which placed much demand on Jamie. She wanted to continue to be my primary caretaker and also always be there for our children. This required a lot of patience on both of our parts but we knew that we wanted their needs to come before ours.

We made a decision that we were content having these two children and didn't want to have more. Having two children required much energy and we wanted to be able to give both of them enough attention without the demands from a third child. Coming from a family of five children myself, I knew that I didn't want a large family of my own. Also, we knew that raising children would be expensive, and at that time we expected that we may not be able to afford more. I was obviously fertile and had the ability to produce children. We could have either chosen to have Jamie's tubes tied or for me to have a vasectomy. We elected the latter and scheduled my surgery. It was unbelievable to think that I was told after my injury years earlier that I would never be able to father children, and now here I was electing to not have any more. It seems quite strange, but I figured that it would not be painful because I did not have sensation in my genitals. After the surgery, I often joked with my friends telling them that I was the only guy able to undergo a vasectomy without the need of any local anesthesia. I often wonder what the chances were that there was another complete spinal cord injured quadriplegic who had a vasectomy performed voluntarily.

I recognized that raising two young children and taking care of a quadriplegic was very demanding on Jamie. I could see the stress that this created, and it did cause a strain on our marriage. I knew that Jamie always loved me, but I feared that she had taken on too many responsibilities. I assume that most relationships are strained when raising young children, but we were different because I relied on her for so much. Even when she knew that she needed help, she was reluctant to ask for it. My mother and her father would make themselves readily available whenever we needed assistance, but she didn't ask often enough.

There were many times that I considered hiring a personal care aide for myself, but Jamie didn't want a stranger coming into our house. I felt that this created a Catch-22 for me because she didn't want another person caring for me, but she was often overwhelmed by the responsibilities involved with our children and my care. When I was an inpatient at the rehabilitation center as a young man, I recall the nursing staff recommending that I have an aide to assist with my personal needs and to not place this burden on a mate. Jamie always wanted to be my primary caretaker and told me that she was happy to do it. I guess at that time it was just her and me alone, but when the additional responsibilities of children came into our lives, it became too burdensome.

For the first time ever, we drifted apart as a couple emotionally but continued to live our lives together physically. I know that she always loved me, but I was insecure worrying that she would find someone else. I imagined that she would find a man that didn't have any physical limitations and would be able to assist her with all of the needs as most husbands do. It was fortunate for me that our love was strong enough that, despite our problems at that time, we stayed together.

Our Traveling Adventures

I have always loved the adventure of traveling and visiting new places. Jamie also enjoyed this and was never fearful of going to unknown sites and having new adventures. As a young couple we drove my accessible van to local attractions and then started flying together on vacations. I loved having a partner who was not fearful of the unknown and was willing to pack up and go when we were able to. We decided that we wanted to experience as much of this as possible with our children. We started taking them with us everywhere that we went, either for work-related purposes or vacations. We always loved having them with us and figured what better way to educate them about new places and different cultures.

It is very difficult traveling with a disability like mine, especially flying. Getting onto a plane requires much assistance from Jamie and the airline staff. I typically roll down the jetway in my own electric chair, and at the end they assist with transferring me into an aisle chair. This is a very narrow seat on small wheels that I am strapped into. It's used to wheel me into the airplane and next to my airplane seat in the aisle. I am then transferred again, typically by two strong guys who can lift me into the aisle seat and strap me in for the airplane ride. My electric wheelchair will then be transported to the baggage section underneath the plane. The airlines will typically put me on first to avoid congestion in the aisle and then I will wait to get off last where this whole process is done in reverse.

Even as young as two years old, we took Brady on his first flight and adventure to a work conference in Tucson, Arizona. While I was at the conference during the day, Jamie would entertain Brady at the hotel pool. In the evenings we would hang out together. He loved being with us and we realized that even though it was difficult for us to travel, it was worth the effort. We would often rent a wheelchair-accessible van in the city we were visiting and use this for transportation. Unfortunately, in the early 1990s, there were not many companies that had accessible vans for rent throughout the country. This often limited where we were able to visit because without a van for transportation, we would not be able to get around. After the ADA was passed in 1991, many cities began to have better accessible public transportation and more private companies began to offer accessible vans for rent.

Our sense of adventure and the ADA allowed us to take trips to Mexico, Canada and the Caribbean, as well as

European cities like Paris, London, Barcelona, Amsterdam, Brussels, Bruges, Copenhagen, many countries throughout the Baltic Sea region and most of the United States, including Hawaii. Jamie's fearlessness as a traveler and my desire to be with her has propelled me to go to destinations that I would have never imagined I would travel to in my lifetime. My brother Jeff often tells me that he is amazed at how we travel to sites all over the world despite my disability. He comments, "My brother never sits still even in a wheelchair!"

During a trip to Hawaii we decided we wanted to view the historic site Pearl Harbor. I was using my portable electric wheelchair that had inflatable tires with an inner tube. While we were in the visitor entry area, I noticed that one of my rear tires seemed low and I became concerned. I brought this to Jamie's attention, and we decided to watch it carefully in hopes that if it was a leak it would be slow and we would have time to complete our visit. Unfortunately, within minutes the rear tire was deflating quickly and was almost completely flat. This made it very difficult for the chair to move with my weight in it, but I was still able to move very slowly and awkwardly. A security guard, who was a military officer there, at the site was gracious enough to push and assist me out to the parking lot and into my van. He gave us directions to the closest location where I would be able to buy a Fix a Flat spray can that could be used to inflate the tire. This was a spray can filled with a mixture of compressed air and a liquid glue that is often used to repair leaks on rubber-tubed tires.

We headed towards the closest Kmart and were able to purchase the spray can that we were looking for. After inserting the solution into the tire it seemed that the flat had been fixed. Unfortunately, the hole in the inner tube must have been larger than we thought and the tire started to go flat again with the repair solution leaking out of the side of the tire. It was obvious that we needed to replace the inner tube but this was not an item that could be easily purchased at any department store. We inquired and were fortunate to locate a durable medical equipment store that sold wheelchairs similar to mine. They had a new inner tube available which we gladly bought.

Coincidentally the store was next to a tire repair shop for cars. It seemed logical that we would be able to have them change the tube and repair the flat in this store. As Jamie and the kids stood waiting, the repair man inserted a tire jack under my wheelchair and propped it up onto one side while I was still sitting in it. What a sight, here I was sitting in my wheelchair with the hydraulic jack under me, feeling like I was a racing car in the pits trying to get out as fast as possible! He began to pump air into the new tube and tire but didn't realize that the force of his air pump was too strong for this small inner tube. Suddenly I heard a loud pop and realized that he had blown up the tube too much and it exploded like a balloon. Here I was, sitting in my wheelchair on a car jack with a second flat tire and again no replacement. I felt like a monument erected in the middle of this auto repair shop. As people walked by the large open garage doors, they stared at me probably because they had never seen somebody in a wheelchair raised up on a car jack. What a way to spend my vacation time in Hawaii!

Jamie headed back to the DME store to purchase another inner tube, but unfortunately we had purchased the last one that they had in stock. We were told that they could have another one brought over from one of their local sister stores, but we would have to wait for it. We had no other options at that time, so despite our frustration, had to impatiently wait for another hour to get a new inner tube delivered. After it was delivered, the car service technician replaced the blown out tube and slowly pumped air into this new one. This time all went well and my flat tire was fixed! The trip had started out so well, but as often happens, we ran into many complications that seem to occur when traveling with a wheelchair and disability.

On a different trip, I ran into a similar problem. We had all taken a trip to Paris to see the sites and culture of this beautiful city. On our return home, we were trying to catch our flight at Charles de Gaulle airport when I noticed that one of the front tires on my wheelchair had quickly lost air and was flat. Driving on a flat front tire is nearly impossible because it impedes my ability to turn. We had checked in but needed to get to our gate. Jamie was loaded up with our carry-on bags and the kids were too small to assist me with my chair. One of the airport service attendants noticed that I was unable to move and walked alongside me while lifting the front corner of my wheelchair so that I could move forward. I knew that this was very difficult for him to do because he was literally bending over at the waist the whole time while walking at least a quarter-mile. We were unable to go very fast, but he knew that we needed to get to the gate and had committed to helping me. We eventually arrived at our gate and I couldn't thank him enough for his consideration. It is times like this that you truly appreciate the kindness of others, especially those willing to help people like me in dealing with the adventures of traveling with a disability.

In the summer of 2001 we took a family vacation to London. When we arrived at our rooms, Jamie plugged my wheelchair battery charger into an electrical wall socket that completely zapped the unit. My wheelchair requires a charge at the end of every day on vacation because we spend so much time sightseeing. Not having a charger meant that the chair would need to be pushed manually, making it extremely difficult for Jamie and not enjoyable for me. We had known that in Europe they commonly use 220 V sockets and that most equipment requires a less powerful 110 voltage currency socket. A converter unit is needed so that the voltage running through the electrical equipment will not be too strong and damaging. She had forgotten this and had not used the converter unit before plugging in the recharger. Ouch! It was a very simple mistake but left us in a bind.

It was fortuitous that when we first came into the hotel, we met a man in an electrical wheelchair similar to mine. We spoke with him briefly and never imagined that we would later ask to borrow his battery charger until we could get another. That worked for the first evening and the next morning we asked our tour guide to take us to a medical equipment store where we could purchase another battery charger. After driving around for several hours we finally found one that had a compatible charger. We purchased it and used it for the remainder of our trip. We were in a very large city that was completely strange to us and had never expected that we would be doing this type of shopping!

Another traveling difficulty for me is that I wear a urine bag that is strapped to my lower leg and attached by a rubber hose to my penis external catheter. I do not have any control of my bladder functions, so this allows me to urinate throughout the day without having to go into a restroom. When I first get up in the morning and into my wheelchair, I always am careful to make sure that the catheter is secured properly and that the hose is not kinked so that there will not be any accidents that result in me having a wet crotch. Unfortunately, this does happen on occasion and makes for a very awkward situation where I need to change the catheter and my pants. When flying I get transferred out of my wheelchair into a transfer chair and then into the airplane seat. Problems can occur during a transfer because I am being lifted and the hose may accidentally get pulled or out of position.

In the summer of 2016 we took a family trip to the Netherlands. Maria's boyfriend (and future husband) Grant joined us. This provided us with a great opportunity to get to know him better and for him to better understand my limitations. It was a wonderful trip and we all truly enjoyed seeing this part of the world, but it ended with an extremely awkward flight home. We had a seven-hour flight to Chicago and then would transfer there to head to Pittsburgh. We were flying out of the Brussels airport waiting to board our plane and were called to the gate. As we were heading towards the ramp, Jamie suddenly exclaimed to me that my pants were wet in my crotch. This was a horrible situation because the plane was ready to be boarded. I would have to board first and get settled before the airline let others onto the plane, so there were many people behind me very anxious to get on and find a seat. Unfortunately, this meant that I was going to have to sit in my wet pants for the complete seven hour flight.

When I was transferred into the aisle chair, I embarrassingly left a puddle on the seat. The flight attendant put a plastic bag down on my airplane seat prior to me being placed there. At least this would keep the seat from getting wet and stop the next passenger from having to sit in a wet spot. After the plane was completely loaded and we were in flight, Jamie placed a blanket over my lap and tried to open my pants with hopes of inconspicuously checking my catheter and correcting the problem. I can only imagine what other passengers were thinking when they saw her hands under the blanket, fumbling around in the dark.

When we arrived in Chicago, we had to quickly change planes which did not give me any time to dry my pants. We looked for the nearest family restroom. These are restrooms designated for use by parents with children or by someone like me that needs assistance from a person of the opposite sex. Unfortunately, there are not many of these and we scrambled to find one available. Finally we found a restroom and Jamie was able to change my external catheter to avoid more urine leaking out on the remaining trip home. It was not possible for her to get me out of my chair to change pants even if I had another pair available. We then flew for another two hours to arrive in Pittsburgh resulting in me spending the whole day in wet pants. This is one of the hazards for me traveling long distances by plane that makes me cautious about these kinds of trips. Looking back now, although the return home was difficult, I would make this trip all over again because I loved spending time traveling with my family.

Growing a Dream

When I took over my father's business in 1991, we had one outpatient facility in Leechburg and one contract with a local skilled nursing facility. We employed four full-time and a few part-time employees. My father had been the primary revenue earner as a treating physical therapist and had also served as the administrator. I was able to come in and take over his role as the administrator but obviously could not replace his skills as a treating physical therapist. It became imperative for me to begin to recruit and hire well-qualified clinicians to service our patients and allow me to begin to grow the business. I recognized at that point that all of our eggs were in one basket with only one location and one contract. In order for the business to afford to pay me as a full-time administrator we would need growth and I was determined to pursue this challenge.

Within weeks of starting my work, one of the two physical therapists approached me and requested a sizable increase in pay. He was already receiving a pay that was above what other employers offered, but he was trying to take advantage of the situation because he knew I was desperate. I held my ground and refused to increase his rate. This led to him resigning his employment and making my situation tougher, but it was the first step I had to take to send a signal that I was here to stay and I was not going to be pushed around.

At that time, there was a shortage of licensed physical therapists in the industry, especially within rural areas like Leechburg. This made it extremely difficult to recruit staff members. I knew that it would be hard to bring experienced therapists into a small company with limited resources and reputation. I was desperate to hire qualified therapists and made several mistakes bringing on people who were not good employees but had current valid licenses. My first mistake was when I hired an older female physical therapist to service the contract we had with the skilled nursing facility. It seemed that she would be a good fit for this role because she was very compassionate about her patients and enjoyed working in geriatrics. The part that I didn't realize — but soon learned — was that she was horrible with documenting her treatment and was negligent in getting paperwork done. This meant that the nursing facility was unable to bill insurance companies for her services and became disgruntled. Her lack of providing required documentation is probably why she had been readily available for our position and was not working with another employer.

After many attempts to rectify her inadequacies, the nursing facility decided that they would find another physical therapy contractor to provide this service to their patients. This meant that we were losing the contract that accounted for a majority of our company's business revenue. My father had always been diligent about providing great care for his patients but also for providing timely and adequate documentation of services. The facility had gotten used to having him in that role and was not going to settle for anything less. I knew that I had made a grave mistake by hiring an employee that wasn't keeping up with expectations while representing my company. Losing this contract was a big loss for us but also forced me to rethink the strategy for our future growth. I decided that I would no longer pursue contracting with skilled nursing facilities and instead would focus all of my attention on growing our business through additional outpatient facilities.

In the early 1990s there were no cell phones or desktop computers with internet access. Growing a business required physically getting out of my office and being visible in person. I wanted to grow my business and I approached it the only way that I knew. I applied the same principles that I had learned and used in my days of wrestling. I set goals and worked as hard as I could to accomplish them, believing in myself and never quitting. Even though working with a physical disability made these objectives much harder, I still applied these same principles and did not let my disability deter me.

I knew that Jamie supported my endeavors and was always there for me. She gave me the confidence to deal with my disability and having her in my life allowed me to often forget my limitations. I would have never been able to accomplish the many things that I did in my career and personal life without her. Over the next 25 years I grew this business to having nearly sixty employees with gross revenue of over $5 million per year. I was proud to be recognized by my Graduate School of Public Health at the University of Pittsburgh by receiving the Distinguished Graduate Award in 2001. It was ironic that this was the same school that initially did not want to admit me because of the concerns with my disability. I was very proud to receive this award, and I attended the ceremony with my mother, Jamie, Brady and Maria. I know that my mother never imagined that I would attain this when I was a nineteen-year-old kid lying in the ICU with a broken neck. I was grateful that Jamie saw my determination when we met and believed in me despite the wheelchair. She never knew what our future would hold together but was always optimistic and had dedicated her life to me and our children. Having my family at this ceremony was a culmination of everything that I had worked so hard for and wanted in this life. I only wished that my father could have been there because his earlier work gave me this opportunity to succeed. The faces of all of them smiling back at me with pride made me truly comprehend the answer to the question that had haunted me for many years, Is Life Fair?

Like Being Hit by a Bus!

Throughout my many years of life I have learned that sometimes things just happen unexpectedly and we have to deal with them. Every day, accidents occur around you that can directly affect your life or the person walking next to you on the street. Think about how many personal injury attorney advertisements you see daily on television, billboards and radio. Using this as a very crude gauge, it is obvious that there is a constant barrage of accidents occurring around us every day, every hour and every minute of our lives. When will one involve you? This is a rather terrifying thought and can make you feel that you are in a waiting game, always worried about when you or a loved one will be the victim. I have always felt that my tragic accident was my turn. It was that moment in my life where maybe God stopped watching over me, and I was vulnerable to injury. After that, I felt that I had paid my dues and filled my quota for severe accidents in my life. The chances of severe tragedy must be extremely reduced once you have been involved in this type of incident, your chances of being involved again diminished greatly.

These are my optimistic beliefs, and they have proved to be true for me, although I had a close call in November 2013. Jamie and I had attended a Pitt basketball game on a Saturday evening at the Peterson Events Center. This facility is located in the heart of Oakland, a Pittsburgh neighborhood that sits on a large hillside. Parking is very limited at the facility and it is necessary for us to use wheelchair parking in an adjacent garage. This requires traveling a short distance across several street crossings in order to get back to our van. At the end of the basketball game, we left "The Pete" and headed out into the chilled air. We began to move briskly along the sidewalk towards the parking garage as we talked about the exciting overtime victory that our team had just unbelievably won after being down by eighteen points in the second half. The sidewalk was crowded with many other pedestrians who were also leaving the game and heading in the same direction as us. We started to cross the street to reach the parking garage, but stopped, noticing that a campus bus had just turned in front of us and was partially blocking the walkway. The rear end of the bus had not fully passed the painted crosswalk. In order to get to the other side of the street we would need to go around the bus, walking/rolling behind the rear. This is something that I typically never do because I am always very cautious about going behind stopped vehicles, knowing that it is difficult for drivers to see me because I sit much lower to the ground than a standing person. However, I noticed that the bus seemed to begin to edge forward which resulted in me and Jamie, along with numerous other pedestrians, to go behind the bus to cross the street.

As we moved behind the bus, I realized that I had made a very grave mistake because Jamie started to yell, "The bus is backing up!" I saw her pounding on the back of the bus trying to get the attention of the driver. Thinking quickly I wanted to steer my wheelchair away from the oncoming bus bumper, but when I made this sudden motion and attempted a change of direction my hand slipped off of the joystick. In a matter of a split-second, the rear bumper of the bus was pushing against the side of my chair. I could hear, "Stop! Stop! Stop!" coming from Jamie and other witnesses, hoping that the bus would not continue in reverse and crush me in my chair. The bumper was jammed into the side of my chair and I could feel the strength of the bus beginning to push me from the side. It seemed that the chair began to rock up on its side but at that instant, as suddenly as it had backed into me, the bus stopped.

As I sat there helplessly, I recall people scrambling around me trying to dislodge my wheelchair and move out of danger. For that split second I was relieved because the bus had stopped, and I could hear the bus engine decelerating. My relief was very short because as quickly as it had stopped,

I heard Jamie yell, "It's backing up again!" She had been behind me in a precarious position next to the bumper and quickly reached across my body to attempt to grab my wheelchair joystick, hoping to move the chair electronically since I was unable to. She had been pounding on the back of the bus and was now standing in between the bus and me. We were both now in jeopardy of being crushed as the bus tried to continue in reverse. Other pedestrians scrambled out of the way as they saw the reverse lights come on again and could hear the engine begin to accelerate. At that point, I could feel the strength of the bus pushing against me and the strong smell of bus exhaust filled my lungs. I sat helplessly looking down into my lap thinking that this is how I will die. At that moment, I was not afraid because I have always felt that God has a purpose for me on this earth which must have involved me living a majority of my life disabled. I felt that this may have been his time to call me and for me to move into the next chapter of my existence.

That moment became very surreal to me because I could hear screaming and feel the terror of what was happening, but I remained calm and felt a strength seeming to surround me. In the moment of facing death, I remember thinking about my daughter Maria and how much she still needed me at this point in her life. She was a college student nearing graduation and still needed parental guidance. My thoughts were not focused on how this massive bus would crush me and my wheelchair. Instead I was thinking about my life on this earth and the many people who I have loved and who have cared about me in return.

As quickly as the screaming started, it suddenly stopped. I could hear Jamie's voice and I realized that she was hugging me and started to cry. I looked up from my lap and into the face of an unknown woman who asked me, "Are you okay?" In her face I could see the terror of what she had witnessed, and I realized that this incident was very scary to everyone around me. She had a look of total horror in her eyes and disbelief about what had just transpired. I looked down again at my body and hesitantly answered, "I'm okay." Not having any sensation in my limbs and trunk, I need to visibly assess my body to determine any type of damage. The bumper might have broken my arm or mangled my leg and I would not have immediate recognition of this unless I was able to see it. I didn't see any signs of damage and began to realize that it was over. I assume I was in a state of shock because I remained calm and became oblivious to others around me. Jamie continued to cry loudly and I could see that she was shaking vigorously. I became more concerned about her than I did about myself. I reiterated to her that I was okay in hopes that she would calm down.

As my senses began to return, I noticed that a police

officer had been called to the scene and began to question me, Jamie and other witnesses. I refused medical treatment because I seemed alright and was relieved to not visit another hospital needlessly. I began questioning myself . *What had just happened? Did I just miss being crushed by the rear end of the bus?* The cold air of the night seemed to disappear as we sat in the middle of the street near the crosswalk. At some point, the police officer asked me to move off of the road, recognizing that we were interfering with other traffic. At first I was fearful that my electric chair would be unable to move because of possible damage by the bus. Much to my surprise, the chair had not been damaged and I was able to turn it on to roll over to the side of the street.

Eventually Jamie and I made our way back to the parking lot and the van. In a state of disbelief, we talked about the incident and how it had affected us. The ride back home that night was about forty-five minutes long and we shared some laughter, tears and an array of emotions. After arriving home, it really started to hit me that I had once again avoided death and possible tragedy to Jamie. Even though it was near midnight, I called our daughter Maria because I just wanted to hear her voice. She was stunned by my story and recognized the severity of the incident because I could not help but cry as I explained it to her. She knows that I am a person that often tries to hide my emotions and am embarrassed by crying. I had trouble explaining the incident to her, but just kept saying that it was very scary. Hearing her voice and knowing that she was safe helped me to find comfort and recognize that God still wanted me on this earth and that my grown children still needed me.

As you go through life and are faced with troubling times, you will ask yourself, "Is Life Fair?" I feel that life is what you make of it. Sometimes it does not treat you well, but only you can decide how you will deal with it. I sometimes use the metaphor that life is a poker game. You are dealt a hand of cards that you have no control over. Some of your cards are good ones and some are bad ones. You have a choice to play out your hand with the cards that you have been dealt or you fold and quit. I have been dealt many good cards in my life, but I have also received many bad cards. It has been my choice to play with the cards that I have and stay in the game, to never quit. This decision has allowed me to live life as a quadriplegic and enjoy many things, while not looking back and envying the things that I do not have. By playing out my hand and not folding, I have been blessed in my life as I have described throughout this book. I would never wish harm or tragedy on any other living human being, but unfortunately accidents that occur every day may cross your path. When misfortune or tragedy come into your life, don't question if it is fair to you. Instead have faith that a power much greater than us is watching. Live life to the best of your ability and good things will come.

Life Comes Full Circle

When I was in my early 50s, I began to notice health issues that were concerning. I would sometimes become very lightheaded and begin to white out if I skipped a meal or went without eating breakfast. I would sometimes come home from work completely exhausted and unable to function, my shoulders and arms feeling heavy. For several years, I simply ignored what could be a medical condition and continued as I always had. Eventually, Jamie demanded that we go to see my primary care doctor and describe what had been happening to me.

Dr. Deborah McFadden asked me numerous questions and said that she suspected I have type II diabetes. Blood tests confirmed what she thought. I was now a diabetic! Diabetes was prevalent in my father's side of the family, but I never expected that this disease would affect me. I always thought that my younger sister and younger brother would become diabetic because they had many of the characteristics that typically lead to this disease. I began to research more about diabetes to learn how to live with it. All recommendations included modifying my diet to moderate my glucose level and to increase exercise. Increasing exercise is impossible for me because I have very limited muscles that I have control over. This meant that modifying my diet was really the only option I had. When I was a wrestler in my youth, I often dieted to qualify for a certain weight class, and this experience made me recognize how difficult it is to lose weight. As a young healthy athlete, I was able to increase my exercise and activity level at least, but now I would have to rely solely on controlling my diet.

It scared me that being a diabetic quadriplegic now presented me with another obstacle that would make life more difficult. I wasn't as concerned about myself but felt that it was not fair to Jamie because she would have to be the one to monitor my daily blood sugar levels and provide me with additional medications. I was already dealing with the multiple medications necessary for my spinal cord injury condition and now would have to add others. Diabetics often lose their feet or lower legs due to the decreased circulation. My spinal cord injury already caused problems with circulation in my lower extremities, and now I would have additional concerns about my decreased blood circulation that could result in amputation. Is life fair?

I had already lost many of the simple joys in life that many people take for granted. I really don't have many hobbies and am not able to actively participate in sports. The activities that I have learned to enjoy the most are spending time with my family, watching sporting events and movies and eating good food in decent restaurants. Don't get me wrong, I have never been a food junkie, but I do look forward to tasting a good meal and the pleasure of trying new dishes. Now my doctor was recommending that I would have to cut out sugars and reduce carbohydrates. This meant limiting white bread, potatoes, pastas and so many of the foods that I enjoy.

Similarly to how I have often handled tough situations, I knew that I had been handed lemons and would need to make lemonade out of them. Dr. McFadden recommended that I begin to see a doctor that specializes in dealing with diabetes, an endocrinologist. I agreed and she provided me with a phone number. When I called to schedule an appointment at the Joslin Diabetes Center, I was informed that the office was located in the former Citizens General Hospital. This was the same hospital in New Kensington that I was transported to after my spinal cord injury and had stayed in for nearly two months after my initial surgeries. The building was no longer an inpatient hospital facility and had only the emergency room and outpatient services available. I had not returned there for many years but was now scheduled to go back due to my diabetes.

When arriving for my first appointment, I was directed to the former entrance of the emergency room that I recall going through in 1978. At that time, I was lying flat on my back but could recall seeing the heavy glass doors and noticing similar lighting. I remembered feeling very scared and hearing the clanging of the wheels from the stretcher as they rolled me through this entrance. Now, I was rolling in under my own steam but as a much older and experienced person. Inside the building, signage directed me through large, wide wooden doors into the Diabetes Center. As I looked around this facility, I began to realize that this converted space was once the ICU. I was directed into an individual exam room that seemed very familiar to me.

I noticed that this small room was the exact room that I had occupied during my stay in intensive care back in 1978. I looked around and recognized exactly where my bed had once been. The only real view I had had was looking at the ceiling while laying on my back in a halo cast. I remembered that there was a window behind my head that let in the morning sun every day. I never was able to look through this window but knew it was there because of the bright sunlight that would stream in. I noticed the small restroom that had been to the right of my bed and recalled my mother often using it during her long stays at my bedside. I could see my father sitting to the side of my bed when he would come in to visit every evening after working long hard days.

My eyes began to tear up as I could feel the emotions and fears I'd experienced in that room, lying there through Thanksgiving and Christmas that year. It was so hard for me to see my parents dealing with my accident and knowing that they had no control over what had happened. I was so lucky to have a family that cared so much about me. I could remember many of my friends stopping in to visit during those days and crying as they stood over my bed and tried to comfort me.I had made it through those days and survived for many years more, creating a life that was valuable to many others. It was surreal to be sitting in the same room that I had once struggled in for life and where I had felt death. This was the same room that I recall lying in when my lungs collapsed and I began to suffocate. I remember having an out-of-body experience where I watched myself in bed being treated by medical staff trying to revive me as I was no longer breathing. I had a view above my bed in the corner watching as I no longer felt any pain or discomfort.

This room that had been my hell on earth was now a completely different environment because Jamie was with me. I was here again but under much better circumstances and not in a state of emergency, but to be treated for my newly-diagnosed diabetes. I saw this as the next stage in my life. It may not be easy, but I was glad to have reached this point where I could look back and recall how far I had come since initially being here. No one knows what the future holds for me, but I am glad that I have experienced this life and can live to tell others about it and hopefully provide inspiration to anyone who may face similar circumstances or any tragedy. Has this life been fair to me? Some may view my life as a difficult journey, but I feel that I have done the best I can with what I was given and it has been an opportunity to prove that life is what you make of it. I hope that my efforts will be viewed positively and remembered by the many people that have been part of it.

Inducted into the Sports Hall of Fame

I unexpectedly received a telephone call from the chairman of a local organization called the Alle-Kiski Sports Hall Of Fame. He told me that I had been selected to become a member of this local organization that recognized reputable athletes who had stood out in their high school, college or professional athletic careers. I was a bit surprised because my wrestling record from high school was very good but there were others who were better, and my college wrestling career had been cut short by my accident. I asked him why they would recognize my wrestling career from over 40 years ago. He told me that the committee wanted to honor me not just because of what I did before my accident but what I had accomplished after it. This answer convinced me to accept their recognition and to become a member of this group.

I realized that I would need to write a speech for the induction ceremony and started to dwell upon my wrestling career along with the discipline that I had learned from this sport and how it ultimately affected the rest of my life. I wanted my family and friends to be there that evening because I was proud to be recognized for something that was considered exceptional. Even though to me, I was always just doing the best that I could, regardless of whether it was wrestling, getting my education, or pursuing and working a productive career. I knew that Jamie was very proud of me. She has always been a person who loves to throw a party. This gave her a perfect reason! She began to get the word out that I was going to be inducted and we ultimately had over 70 people at the event there to see me. I never knew I had so many friends. I began my speech with one of my favorite quotes, "The older we get, the better we were!" This seemed most appropriate for me and the other eleven inductees there that night. I spoke briefly about my wrestling career but mostly about my life afterward and how I was able to find happiness and success despite the tragic accident. I have learned that life is not easy and at some point all of us will face adversity. Adversity will come in many forms. This unpredictable journey that we call life can be very tough. Everyone faces challenges; it is how you deal with them that will define your character.

I explained that throughout my wrestling career I accomplished most of my goals through discipline, dedication and determination. I learned from these principles that the harder I worked, the more gratifying was my success. Any failure inspired me to work even harder and helped me to recognize that anything was within my grasp as long as I never quit. I discussed these principles that have helped to guide me in my life:

1. **Set goals and believe that you can achieve them with hard work and determination.** Start small with your goals and achieve one at a time before you move on to the next. Achieving your goals will help you to be successful and feel gratified throughout your life.

2. **Make the most of what you have been given.** Many of the inductees have been given a gift of superior athleticism or extreme drive that won't let them quit. The point is that everyone is different and has different qualities. Whatever that quality may be, it is up to you to focus it and use it throughout your life. I believe that it is better to focus on your abilities rather than dwell upon things that you do not have.

3. **Working hard is necessary for you to be successful in whatever you choose.** Understand that working hard can help you to overcome many tough situations. It can level the playing field for those who are not as gifted. It can bring success to many who are willing to push themselves, and it will help you to develop confidence in yourself.

4. **Don't quit!** I am able to look back and remember

how devastating the future looked when I was very young. Here I am now, at the age of 60, extremely happy that I have been blessed with a life of fulfillment and accomplishments.

My eyes welled with tears many times throughout the speech, especially when I spoke about my family. Jamie, Brady and Maria were sitting at a table in front of me and I could see their faces. When I brought up Maria's name, I looked at her eyes and she was crying. I realized that everything I had done as a father and husband was worthwhile because the people that I loved the most appreciated me for it.

After the ceremony, Jamie invited all of our family and friends who had attended over to our house for a celebration. It was a great evening that I will never forget!

Living with a Disability

Sometimes, I honestly feel resentful about becoming physically disabled and not being able to enjoy life the way many others do. At other times, I feel that I was very fortunate to have been able to experience almost 20 years of my life being healthy and physically-gifted. I wonder where I would have ended up if I did not have my accident and what my life would have held. It was a blessing that I was able to be a very physically active boy with memories to cherish. I often think about the little things in my life that I previously enjoyed the most but now cannot. Being able to feel the touch of holding someone's hand, walking barefoot through soft grass, easily sliding out of bed in the morning for a long stretch, feeling warm water running over my body while taking a shower, the gentle ache of sore muscles the day following a vigorous workout, the feel of deeply inhaling and exhaling cold air on a crisp day, the overwhelming sensation of having an orgasm, riding my bicycle and feeling the exhilaration of pedaling for as long as I could or something as simple as driving my car and feeling in control at the wheel and a sense of independence. As Julie Andrews sang, in the film, *The Sound of Music,* "These are a few of my favorite things".

It's a Catch-22. I enjoy thinking of these things but am regretful that I can no longer have them. On the other hand, at least I was able to experience and enjoy many things during the first nearly twenty years of my life that would have been impossible for someone born with a disability. Is it better to have enjoyed those years of normal life and have the memories or is it better to have never had the opportunity to experience them? Is life fair? I guess my answer to this never-ending question is a matter of perspective. Doesn't it all truly depend on how you live your life and deal with what God has presented to you?

I still dread every year when November comes and I begin to think about that one day in the middle of the month that will constantly haunt me. That damned day of November 15! I mostly try not to dwell on it, but the closer it gets the more it becomes reality again. I think back on being a young man so blessed to have the physical abilities that I took for granted. It hurts when I remember that day because I often wonder how different my life would've been if I didn't have that accident. If I had only chosen to go somewhere else that night and not head to the YMCA for wrestling practice. If I had only left the gymnasium two minutes sooner and walked downstairs, not lingering behind. If I had only decided to not do a Granby roll and instead use one of the many other moves that I knew to escape. A change in any one of these decisions would have completely shaped my life differently. What career would I have pursued? Who would I have married? Would I have had children? What would these people have been like? Would I have done anything harmful to others or would I have been helpful? I guess only God knows.

This is the day of the year that I think about Pat, the guy that jumped on top of me, and what he is doing with his life. He came around to see me for a short time after my injury, but I have not seen him in many years and only hear about him through mutual friends that stay in touch. Many people ask me how he felt about the accident and wonder how it affected him. I assume that the reason he never stayed in touch with me is because it hurt him to see me in my condition and know that he was responsible. I honestly don't know this because we never talked about it, but I think that he did have much difficulty in facing the reality of what had happened. The kind side of me does not blame him for my injury because I know that he was young and not very sensible and did not do it on purpose. But the less kind side of me wishes just briefly that he could know a little bit of my pain because he walked away without ever apologizing or expressing any remorse to me. I am resentful that he chose to move away from our area and pursue a normal life, while I was forced to deal with my disability and the difficulties I have in my life.

I guess it is a day that I dread because when it comes I relive in my mind much of the pain and suffering that I have endured since I was nineteen years old. Typically, I am not a person to live in the past because I know that it can't be changed. I live trying to make the most out of every day because I remind myself that tomorrow may never come. I understand that my life will be what I make of it and try to concern myself only with what I can control, not what I can't.

No one ever said that life was going to be fair. What is fairness? Is it fair that some people are born with physical traits that make them exceptional athletes while others are born with very limited physical capabilities? Is it fair that some are born with genius intellect and others are born with developmental disabilities? I feel that I was fortunate to have been born with above-average intelligence and good physical abilities. I was unfortunate to have my physical abilities taken away from me. Is it fair to me? Life is what you make of it. I learned discipline in my first 20 years of life through my involvement with sports, particularly wrestling. I used that self-discipline after my accident to keep myself on track to do the best that I could with what skills I still had. My mind had not been altered so my ability to succeed was still intact. I just needed to pursue it in a different manner. I am very thankful that I had those limited years to play sports — compete in wrestling, learn to swim, ride a bike — and grow up with my peers, develop into a young man and develop a sense of self-confidence that would help me after my accident.

When the rehabilitation team at the rehab center wanted me to have discussions with a psychologist, I refused the sessions because I could not understand why I would need to address my mental health. I guess I thought that my body had been broken, but my mind was still strong. I don't feel a psychologist or the use of counseling isn't beneficial to people that have problems or challenges that they are trying to deal with. It's just that I never wanted to accept that this physical disability would affect my mental outlook and spirit. However, there are many days that I hate being physically disabled and ask the same question that many others do when facing a tragedy in their lives, "Why me?" I don't know the answer to this and I guess if I did I would have the power to have avoided my accident and change the course of my life. Did God allow me to become a quadriplegic so that I could prove to others that living this way can still be very fulfilling? Is it my purpose to assist others and help make their lives better? Whatever the reason, I know that it is often difficult but I am hopeful that others may look at me and recognize that their lives can be better too by never giving up and making the most of every single day.

A Note from Jamie

I can clearly remember seeing Brian "speeding" around the halls of Harmarville Rehabilitation Center when I began working there in the summer of 1985 as a vocational rehabilitation counselor. I was quite fortunate to be hired, in spite of a lack of experience, at what was then one of the most prestigious physical rehabilitation hospitals in all of the United States. HRC was always bustling and busy as you strolled down the Mall, the main hallway, from a physical therapy gym to the outside vocational building where I worked. There were many post-stroke, amputee, head injured and spinal cord injured patients making their way to therapy and scheduled medical appointments with volunteers in red jackets pushing their wheelchairs, carts and even beds along. When I saw a dark-haired, young and very handsome guy in a nicely-tailored suit with shiny dress shoes in an electric wheelchair who looked much more sophisticated and sure of himself than the patients in their sweatpants and T-shirts, I couldn't help but notice. He was definitely someone I wanted to meet!

I watched him sometimes in the cafeteria which was

used by both the staff and the patients who were able to eat independently or with a little assistance from therapists or nurses. I would eat lunch with my newly-hired boss and friend Debbie (Boots) Kuntz or some of my coworkers. Brian would mostly be sitting alone at a table eating with a specially-designed adaptive fork. I also noticed him sitting at a modified desk in the administrative offices when I passed by and had heard that he was being mentored by the president and CEO, Mr. Lee Lacey. We said hello sometimes when he would hear my heels clicking along on the cement floors outside of his desk area, as I was always in high gear to get to my patient appointments. I figured he may not know many people there and since Debbie and I were new to our jobs, I decided to ask if he wanted to eat lunch with us instead of alone. This was the start of our relationship.

I was eager to get to know him, He was so brave and strong, I could just tell. I found him shy and naïve about dating, but he had a sense of humor that made me laugh and laugh. I think that is his best quality! He makes people feel very comfortable around him which makes it easy to get to know him. Once you meet Brian Jacob, you almost certainly will remember him! And people do remember him. He is such a loyal and kind friend to people of all walks of life, and he cares about others so much more than he wants people to worry about him.

When he was in his late 20s, he always used to say to me that he didn't like when people looked at him in his wheelchair or asked him about his accident and why he was in the chair. I would say to him, "It's because you're so well-dressed and look so healthy". He was always so picky about his appearance. He was particular about his pants seams being straight and his feet being strapped to his footrest perfectly and his tie being centered and his hair brushed and parted just so. But he also found humor in their curiosity about his situation and most times he would make up funny stories about what happened to him to see if they would believe him and laugh along with him. "I fell out of a tree," he would say or "I was a racecar driver and had a wreck." The funniest one to me was when the kids and I were slowly pushing him backwards down a long, steep ramp off of a cruise boat. A crew member was very curious about what had happened to Brian and was watching him as he was being guided down the ramp. He asked with his foreign accent and not-so-good English, "What happened to you?" Brian always being the jokester, said to him very seriously, "I was going down this long, long ramp..." leaving the man very perplexed by what he was hearing.

So our dating began quickly... like we had no time to lose! We saw each other at work during the day and made plans to go out in the evenings or over the weekends. We would even sneak in some innocent kisses in the elevator at Harmarville when heading to the second floor! It was great that we liked so many of the same things, like going to the theater, sports of any kind, concerts or art exhibits. We even bought some original art to decorate the new condominium that Brian had bought for himself and his mother.

Our love of sports took us to events all over the US. We began to travel together and there was much for me to learn about quadriplegia, wheelchairs, accessibility, modified vans and such. Luckily, I had made friends with some of the therapists and nurses I worked with at Harmarville and started learning more about spinal cord injuries – and Brian. His father would take us out to dinner on weekends and we would visit him at his house, or his mother would come with us on a trip and we learned about each other easily. I was always very close to my parents, and they never questioned me about dating someone who had a severe disability like Brian had. I actually began to think about this when our daughter was engaged, that it was comforting to think that my mom and dad did not have any doubts about whether I would be able to live a happy and fulfilled married life with Brian. He asked me to marry him after only four months of dating! Crazy, huh? I think we just knew we were going to be together. My parents were very religious and my mom told me often that God would take care of Brian and me through the hard times. I know there were times when I looked to God for strength and comfort, and I think He was with me many, many of those times.

When we first were going to get married, Brian had personal care attendants who came in the mornings to dress him and take him to work or to assist at night or on the weekends. He wanted to keep them after we got married to not make my life different from the "normal" wife. But, as we grew closer to our commitment of marriage, I knew that I wanted to take care of him alone so that our mornings and nights could be just like any other married couples – to sleep in if we wanted to and not have to be on schedule or just be able to be there to help him if he was sick. I felt it was important to our relationship that we keep a bit of our privacy in our family life. I knew it was going to be a very serious commitment, and we told each other that even if we argued or were mad at each other, I would still be there each morning and night to get him in and out of bed as it could not be a question. There were days when we didn't speak to each other, but mostly this helped strengthen our love or end the argument a bit faster because we both knew we were there for each other each and every day.

This became especially important when we had our children, Brady and Maria. I really tried to make it like a "normal" home life as they grew up. Brian and I tried to give them everything that they needed, and we wanted them to know how much we love them. They were surely the greatest gifts of our lives. True miracles from God! I also believe that having these two sweet people and their love in our lives helps keep Brian healthy and gives him strength and purpose in his work every day. Family memories and time spent together as the four of us became most important of all. It's been wonderful having those two call us Mom and Dad.

To say it was a total surprise when Brian and I found out I was pregnant with Brady is an understatement! On one of those many long and lonely days in the hospital or rehab center, Brian must have silently prayed to God and asked him for this miracle. Dr. Brenes and all the spinal cord doctors working with Brian had already told him that his paralysis was complete and irreversible and that one of the many things he lost that day in 1978 was the ability to father his own children. Or so they said! As we prepared for a child while living in North Carolina, we knew it would be better for all of us to move back home to Pennsylvania. Hurricane Brady came into our lives a few weeks before the real Hurricane Hugo hit our house in Hickory, NC in August 1989. It was a day that we will never forget. We never felt more blessed than we did holding that little child in our arms and realizing that he is here on this Earth for us to love forever.

Brian was an unbelievable father. He patiently waited for me to assist him in the mornings and nights while I cared for Brady. Since I was not working at the time, he knew he was the provider for the family but that was not enough for him. He figured out ways to take care of Brady and feed him bottles, tell him stories about make-believe Benny, and be the "stroller" when we went out. Brady would stand on Brian's footrest and face him, holding onto the side pieces, so I never really had to put him in a stroller.

We moved to Pittsburgh when Brady was six weeks old, so we had lots of family babysitters around and enjoyed every minute of our new role as parents. As Brady grew, he and his father had a special relationship, two buddies. They both share that dry sense of humor and are constantly teasing and poking fun at each other – and me and Maria! Brady was a very bright child with a strong curiosity that Brian fueled with stories of sports and what was going on at his business. He even taught him how to follow the stock market.

One of the sweet times I had watching them interact was when Brady was innocently studying how his dad did things at home. Brady was a toddler and stayed close to Brian's side at all times. Brian, the "man of the house", had the TV remote always near him, resting on his lap. Since Brian's fingers were flaccid due to his quadriplegia, he used the side of his hand to press down on the buttons. So, as Brady tried to change the channel on the TV for his dad, he picked up the remote from his lap and then turned his little chubby hand on its side, mimicking the way that his dad did this rather than making use of his fingers. He assumed that this is the way it works!

The two follow Pittsburgh sports teams like the Pittsburgh Penguins passionately, and they rarely miss Pittsburgh Pirates baseball games live or on TV. They are always talking baseball statistics and players. Brian always attended Brady's own sporting events through the years – tennis, squash, baseball, or youth wrestling. I would pick Brian up from work and we would not miss being there to cheer him on for any reason. Many, many times Brian would not be feeling well, but I doubt Brady would have ever known as Brian would never let him down and not be in the stands to watch him.

Having a daughter who was as caring and shy as Maria also brought out the best in Brian. Becoming a father for the second time was, again, miraculous and unbelievable. Having a little girl softened Brian and motivated him to make sure that we would all be taken care of if something happened to him. He loves everything about her and she quickly became "Daddy's little girl". When she was sick or scared, he was always by her side to comfort her. When she was born, in January 1992, I usually had to pack up a newborn, a two-and-a-half-year-old with all his gear and Brian in order to go to the store to get groceries, diapers, formula, and everything else in all kinds of weather. I was going around the grocery store with Brady and Maria in the shopping cart when an older woman seemed to stare at me and asked how old Maria was. I told her that she was only one week old, and the woman said, "You shouldn't have her out in this kind of weather at that age!" I was shocked at the woman's opinion of this. I was doing the best I could at the time, and I would never do anything to harm my precious family.

The night before Maria's first day of third grade, she fell off her bike and broke her leg at the baseball field where Brady was having Little League practice. I helped her into bed that night with her cast causing her such pain, and Brian and I stayed for a long time in the room until she fell asleep. Afterwards, Brian did not want to go to sleep. He sat next to her in his wheelchair as he wished for some way to ease her pain. He helped her get used to her small red wheelchair that she had to use for the first few weeks and made her smile and laugh. He used to chase her around the house and she would cry out because, with his motorized chair, he was much faster than she was! She grew up knowing that her dad was always going to be there for her. He and I both (along with many others) taught her to drive, and she ended up with many fender benders. Brian didn't have his driver's license after his accident, but he would take her out driving when she was a new driver. She would sideswipe his accessible van on the curb and bends. He would later come home and chuckle about these moments. Only Maria could get away with this from him!

I believe the best lesson that the kids learned from their father was to have discipline and strength at all times. He taught them to not become discouraged if things did not fall their way. He taught them battle hard and you will succeed. Many people in Lower Burrell thought Brian was a successful person and he had become comfortable in life because his father had left him some of his inheritance and his small physical therapy business. That is true but, they didn't realize that Brian had grown the business to become what it is today —a profitable business made up of nine outpatient centers and a separate home health agency — by applying his business and health care degrees and by being present at work full time for 30+ years. Brian never applied for government or Social Security disability benefits, although we knew he would be able to receive these due to the permanency of his injury. We relied mainly on his income and the medical insurance that he paid for through the company for all of his medical, drug and wheelchair expenses. We often had to budget for a new accessible van or pay out-of-pocket for many of his supplies and medical needs. He was proud to make it on his own and we were lucky we had enough money to raise our family comfortably and pay for their college educations and such. Brady and Maria saw their father and mother work hard every day to provide for them, and we lovingly gave them as much as we could.

I know it is hard to imagine that someone who is as permanently and totally disabled as Brian is the one in our family who took care of all of us, including his mother and siblings in many ways, but it is the truth. It is remarkable to say that he strived every day to complete his daily goals at work and at home with never ending persistence and determination. After I would get him in his wheelchair every morning, he would always kiss me and tell me that he loved me, and he would be off to the races! He never stopped until I put his head back on the pillow at night. On many, many occasions he was sick or hurting or his autonomic dysreflexia was so severe that anyone else would have pulled the covers up over their head and stayed in bed all day. But, not Brian, not my amazing husband, my Bunches. I cannot remember more than a few days in the thirty-four years that we have been married, that I heard him complain about getting up and starting his day, which on most days began at

6:00 AM.

Brian and I had a normal routine to start and end every day of our many married years since 1987. I used to tease him and say to him, "You wear the pants in the family, but I am the one who puts them on you!" We both dealt with our situation with laughter and *our* normal which was full of love and commitment to each other.

"Strength does not come from physical capacity. It comes from an indomitable will." – Mahatma Gandhi

About the Author

Since the age of 19, Brian Jacob has lived his life as a quadriplegic. He wrote his memoir to share chapters of his life's story and inspire other individuals that face any tragedy. His book reflects his acceptance of unfair circumstances that led him on an amazing journey with many joyful moments that ultimately brought him to a place of peace.

Brian was born in Gardner, Massachusetts and raised in New Kensington, Pennsylvania in a dysfunctional but loving family. His love of the sport of wrestling throughout his youth developed his character, discipline and determination. Unfortunately, it was his involvement in this same sport that resulted in a tragic spinal cord injury and permanent disability.

His pursuit of further education and employment led to the fortuitous meeting of his future wife, Jamie Gaydos. Their relationship and life together is described throughout the memoir. It reflects that despite extreme difficulties, life ultimately can be fair. Especially as it relates to love.

Brian currently lives in Lower Burrell, Pennsylvania with Jamie. Together they have lovingly raised their children, Brady and Maria. With Jamie's support throughout this time, Brian successfully developed many outpatient rehabilitation facilities and a home health agency. He continues to actively manage these businesses with the assistance of his son and devoted staff.

At the top of the Duquesne Incline overlooking Pittsburgh, Pennsylvania, with my family on my 60th birthday and 41 years after my spinal cord injury.

Made in the USA
Columbia, SC
24 July 2022

63821397R00162